PALGRAVE POCKET CONSULTANTS

Palgrave Pocket Consultants are concise, authoritative guides that provide actionable solutions to specific, high-level business problems that would otherwise drive you or your company to employ a consultant. Written for aspiring middle to senior managers working across business at any scale, they offer solutions to the most cutting-edge issues across modern business. Be your own expert and have the advice you need at your fingertips.

Available titles:

ATTRACTING AND RETAINING TALENT
Tim Baker

MYTH-BUSTING CHINA'S NUMBERS
Matthew Crabbe

Forthcoming titles:

THE NEW CHINESE TRAVELER
Gary Bowerman

THE WORKPLACE COMMUNITY
Ian Gee and Matthew Hanwell

MANAGING ONLINE REPUTATION
Charlie Pownall

CREATING A RESILIENT WORKFORCE
Ivan Robertson and Cary Cooper

Series ISBN 9781137396792

About the Author

Jeremy Gordon has worked with government departments, financial institutions, and major corporates on strategy, risk, and business development in China for over 20 years. Initially in Hong Kong as an officer with Britain's Brigade of Gurkhas (where his first experience of Chinese officialdom was coming face-to-face with an armed officer on board a suspected smugglers' boat), he later gained China trade, investment, and consulting experience with a diversified Hong Kong based group, and went on to establish the consulting company China Business Services in 2002.

He has been the Honorary Secretary and a Committee Member of the 48 Group Club, and a UK Trade & Investment Business Specialist for mainland China, Taiwan, and Hong Kong. He is Director of China Edge, a consultancy focused on Chinese consumers, and a trustee of Mothers' Bridge of Love, a charity that supports disadvantaged Chinese children.

He lives in London with his wife and their two children.

A Guide to Due Diligence

Risky Business in China

Jeremy Gordon

palgrave
macmillan

First published 2014 by
PALGRAVE MACMILLAN

Palgrave Macmillan in the UK is an imprint of Macmillan Publishers Limited, registered in England, company number 785998, of Houndmills, Basingstoke, Hampshire RG21 6XS.

Palgrave Macmillan in the US is a division of St Martin's Press LLC, 175 Fifth Avenue, New York, NY 10010.

Palgrave Macmillan is the global academic imprint of the above companies and has companies and representatives throughout the world.

Palgrave® and Macmillan® are registered trademarks in the United States, the United Kingdom, Europe and other countries.

ISBN 978–1–137–43321–3

This book is printed on paper suitable for recycling and made from fully managed and sustained forest sources. Logging, pulping and manufacturing processes are expected to conform to the environmental regulations of the country of origin.

A catalogue record for this book is available from the British Library.

A catalog record for this book is available from the Library of Congress.

Typeset by MPS Limited, Chennai, India.

Contents

List of Figures and Tables

Figures

Tables

List of Abbreviations and Acronyms Used

ACFTU – All-China Federation of Trade Unions
AIC – Administration of Industry and Commerce (China)
AMC – Asset management companies
AML – Anti-Monopoly Law
BRICs – Brazil, Russia, India, China
CBBC – China-Britain Business Council
CCTV – China Central Television
CEIBS – China Europe International Business School
CLW – China Labour Watch
CPC – Communist Party of China (The Party)
CPPCC – Chinese People's Political Consultative Conference
CRM – Customer Relationship Management
CSR – Corporate Social Responsibility
CTMO – China Trade Mark Office
EHSS – Environmental, Health, Safety and Social
EIAL – Environmental Impact Assessment Law
EPL – Environmental Protection Law
ERP – Enterprise resource planning
ESG – Environmental, social and corporate governance
EU – European Union
EUCCC – European Chamber of Commerce in China
FCPA – Foreign Corrupt Practices Act
FYP – Five-Year Plan
GAC – General Administration of Customs of China
HKSE – Hong Kong Stock Exchange
HR – Human Resources

ICRIS – Integrated Companies Registry Information System (Hong Kong)
IPR – Intellectual Property Rights
M&A – Mergers and Acquisitions
MEP – Ministry of Environmental Protection (China)
MOFCOM – Ministry of Commerce (China)
MOJ – Ministry of Justice (China)
NAFTA – North American Free Trade Agreement
NBS – National Bureau of Statistics (China)
NPC – National People's Congress (China)
NPLs – Non-performing loans
PBoC – People's Bank of China
PSB – Public Security Bureau (China)
QC – Quality Control
SAIC – State Administration of Industry & Commerce (China)
SAT – State Administration of Taxation (China)
SEC – Securities and Exchange Commission
SEPA – State Environmental Protection Administration (China)
SFDA – State Food and Drug Administration (China)
SIPO – State Intellectual Property Office (China)
SME – small and medium enterprises
SOE – State-owned enterprise
SOX – Sarbanes-Oxley
SPC – Supreme People's Court (China)
TPIs – Third Party Intermediaries
USCBC – US-China Business Council
VAT – Value Added Tax
VIE – Variable Interest Entity
WTO – World Trade Organization

Acknowledgments

Many people have helped with the development of this book, some of them over many years of working experience and others during the commissioning, research, and editing. I am grateful to Old China Hand (and best-selling author) Paul French for introducing the project, and to Tamsine O'Riordan and Josephine Taylor at Palgrave Macmillan for their support in its development.

A number of experienced China business people with specialist areas of expertise were kind enough to share their insights for the book, and a special thanks is due to: Andrew Hupert of China Solved; Arie Schreier of PTL Group; Chris Cheung and Ludmila Hyklova of the EU China Centre; Dan Harris of Harris Moure (and China Law Blog); David Cogman of McKinsey; David Dayton of Silk Road International; Fons Tuinstra of the China Speakers' Bureau; Guy Olivier Faure of China Europe International Business School; Hai Yang of Beijing Steele Investigations; Kent Kedl of Control Risks; Kerry Brown of University of Sydney; Katherine Peavy of Cross Pacific Partner; Lui Kam and Bruno Bensaid of Shanghaivest; Mark Schaub, Liu Xiangwen, Xia Dongxia, and Li Xiny of King & Wood Mallesons; Mark Kitto, author of China Cuckoo; Matthew Crabbe of Mintel; Nathan Li of Kelly Services; Paul Gillis of Guanghua School of Management at Peking University; Piers Touzel of ERM; Rebecca Palser of The Risk Advisory Group; Renaud Anjoran of Sofeast; Richard Brubaker of Collective Responsibility and China Europe International Business School; Rupert Utley of Censere; Seth Peterson of Heidrick & Struggles; Stefan Kracht of Fiducia

Management Consultants; Suwei Jiang of PwC; W. John Hoffmann of Exceptional Resources Group; and Weng Yee Ng of Forensic Risk Alliance.

My family also deserves a massive shout-out for their patient support, and for allowing me to shut the office door and burn the midnight oil.

Introduction

Risk is a major reason that companies fail in, or fail to enter, China. But, as the business pages of the world's newspapers proclaim on an almost daily basis, business risk is a global phenomenon that cannot easily be constrained by borders, rules, or regulators. Risky business is not about geographies. Whether it is in China or anywhere else, risk is an integral part of any business, and one that all managers need to address. But different markets present different risks, and require different approaches. It is up to individual managers and business owners to assess, accept, and manage those risks in a way that suits their moral, operational, and regulatory requirements.

While risk is a simple business reality, it is not always a simple thing to manage. As China is such a large market, with a lot at stake for many businesses, those normal business risks can be amplified—China may be a primary source of a company's materials or products, or the location of its main manufacturing base. It may be a key market, the main source of growth, or the focus for future development. Or all of the above. Risk in China demands a closer look, and the looking needs to be done with eyes wide open and feet firmly on the ground.

Since my feet first hit the ground in Hong Kong way back in 1987, I have been lucky to have travelled (for business and pleasure) across much of China. Like anyone who has experienced this period of dynamic growth, in addition to the crowded trains and dusty roads, there also seems to have been an element of time travel involved—the Beijing of today, from the airport to downtown, seems a hundred years away from the Beijing of the early 1990s, and the same can be said of places across the country. Remember Shanghai before Pudong? Dali before the airport? Shopping with Foreign Exchange Certificates (FECs)?[1] The pace of change continues to surprise, and is a constant reminder for the need to stop, look around, and recalibrate on a regular basis.

On my China travels I have drunk many toasts (including at a wintery breakfast on a Heilongjiang farm!), eaten all manner of food at roadside carts and official banquets (for the record, no more sea cucumber please), sung in karaoke bars (enough said), toured dirty old (and gleaming new) factories, met with all levels of local and central government officials (with all levels of success), and with an amazing variety of business people (though resisting the urge to name-drop here). On this journey I have variously been shocked, frustrated, exhausted, excited, entertained, and inspired—a strangely refreshing, and very Chinese, cocktail of emotions. Along the way I have also learnt a few lessons which I hope can help others experience some of what China has to offer, while avoiding some of the risks.

This book is based on over 20 years of personal experience dealing with business strategy and risk management in China for companies ranging from multinationals to SMEs, and from listed companies to family-owned businesses—sometimes helping with crisis recovery (that could often have been avoided with a little up-front due diligence), and sometimes helping spot, and plot a course around, the red warning flags. The book focuses on the risks faced by foreign companies (which are, in reality, just teams of fallible human beings) dealing with, or working in, China. It demonstrates that due diligence is an essential part of the business adventurer's toolkit and that, properly applied—ranging from simple, DIY processes to complex investigations and strategic decision-making—it cannot only reduce business risk but also provide excellent business intelligence to support negotiations and to build successful business relationships—and businesses.

chapter 1

Opportunity and Risk

A balancing act

The opportunity to do business and make money in China has been on the mainstream corporate agenda for over 20 years, but in that time the nature of the opportunities has fundamentally changed—as have the risks. In an ironic reversal of the "China is risky" school of thought, it was the China opportunity that was suddenly brought into focus following the global financial crisis of 2008—as "mature" economies suffered from the impact of massive, previously unseen, systemic risks in the financial markets.

While most developed economies suffered painful reversals, China was relatively unscathed in terms of its banking system (but that's a subject for another book!). It also offered unparalleled opportunity for growth—fuelled by the government's fixed-asset investment and a fiscal stimulus spending plan totalling some RMB4 trillion (US$586 billion). China's massive infrastructure spending program got a lot of attention, but China offered corporates much more. One of China's key economic policy aims is to rebalance the economy away from its traditional model of export-driven growth and fixed-asset investment, and towards a more sustainable, consumption-driven growth model. The impact of this policy shift had already started to be felt by the time of the financial crisis, and was enhanced by new developments, including expansion of healthcare insurance provisions to over 95 per cent of the population, increasing minimum wages, and the strong emergence of China's consuming middle class.

Opportunities and risks should not be viewed in isolation but as balancing forces that are in constant flux. The rewards of any market or business opportunity always need to be set against the risks—and those risks change from place to place, and over time. They are also hard to define in absolute terms, so businesses have to rely on a mixture of corporate process, data, and personal perception to try and ensure a three-dimensional view and a sensible balance that results in a positive outcome. A manager tasked with following the process and making the judgment has to rely on experience and the available information. Where process, experience, or information is lacking, the risks rapidly increase. Add in external, China factors such as fast-changing markets, policies and regulations, opaque information, and a challenging legal environment, as well as internal, corporate ones such as far-off head offices, tight deadlines, career pressures, lack of resources, and a light-touch approach to corporate governance, and there is a recipe for disaster.

The widely-referenced 1990's book, "Mr. China,"[1] entertainingly highlighted the risks faced by early investors charging into uncharted Chinese territory, waving large amounts of American money around. The results were, with the benefit of hindsight, rather predictable. These stories, and others, influenced a generation of international managers, making many believe that China was inherently risky. There were, and remain, an abundance of risk factors in China, but it was often the business process as much as the business environment that allowed the risks to overtake the rewards. And of course, the success stories don't make for such compelling reading!

Despite the variety, Big Risks are generally Very Visible. Unfortunately this often gives managers confidence that they can get around them with a small change of direction. But risks can also be a bit like icebergs, and while the tip can be seen, and easily avoided, many businesses and projects (even those that are not Titanic in scale) end up sinking because nobody bothered to look below the surface, where the bulk of the risk was hidden—despite the fact everyone knows that fraudsters try their best to hide their frauds! In some markets, like China, the waters may be neither calm nor clear, complicating matters further. So someone has to get their hands dirty.

Due diligence provides that under-the-surface safety check, and can go a long way to identifying and quantifying risks, and allowing for them to be mitigated. It is also a massively under-utilized risk management tool in China. There are a number of reasons for this. It is often mis-understood as being:

• The domain of shady spooks
• An unnecessary cost
• Too time-consuming
• Insulting to an important partner
• A blockage to a big deal
• A wasted investment if no "dirt" is found

Proper due diligence should be used as part of any sensible business or investment planning. The question managers should be asking them-selves is not *whether* to do due diligence, but *when* to do it. Directors and stakeholders should ensure that processes are in place to get the right sort of due diligence done, and directors should take the results seriously—as some "opportunities" are best left alone. The alternative is to bear the consequences should things go wrong. That is all part of business life, and things will sometimes end badly. The problem is that the individual risk taker is usually not the consequence bearer—especially in a market like China where far-away, senior management may delegate a lot of decision-making authority to locally employed staff (whether Chinese or foreign). In some cases the risk taker may benefit from all the upside (bonuses and promotions on the back of successful deals), but little or none of the downside (meaning pain for shareholders and potential implications for directors). Processes for the performance and review of due diligence are therefore a critical ingredi-ent in the management of risk.

The level of due diligence actually performed will depend on the level of, and appetite for, risk. But risks are perceived differently by different people, different organizations, and in different cultures, and the outcomes are due as much to the location in which they exist (China, for example) as to the attitude, approach, and skill of the people who take them (you, dear reader!).

This book highlights some of the key risks international businesses face in China, and seeks to help managers navigate through them with some practical due diligence processes and tools—bringing the balance back in favor of the rewards, and the huge business opportunity that the China market presents.

Risky Business in Brief: A Balancing Act

- *China is not uniquely risky but its size and importance amplifies the risks*
- *Old assumptions don't address new realities (and "old" can be quite recent)*
- *Management processes, information and experience need to be China-relevant*
- *Due diligence is not just for multinationals nor it is conducted by shady spooks*
- *Less due diligence really does mean more risk*

China risk in context

Big, Western businesses have a long history of corporate scandals stretching back to the Medici Bank collapse (1494) and the South Sea Bubble (1720).[2] But there are plenty of more recent cases ... from bad bets and bribes to outright frauds, the likes of Enron, Siemens, GSK, WorldCom, Parmalat, Madoff, and Lehman Brothers, to name just a few, are reminders that business risk is real around the world. If even big, blue-chip companies, with sophisticated management systems, operating in highly regulated markets, under the watchful eyes of external auditors, bank analysts, shareholders, and regulators can fall foul of risk, then there is no room for complacency anywhere. When operating away from home markets, and in the context of new employees, operations, investments, partners, or technologies, the risks are obviously amplified. Even where business operations are overseas, the corporate risk may lie in another country, for example where UK or US authorities initiate Bribery Act or Foreign Corrupt Practices Act (FCPA) investigations. Risks cross borders with impunity.

As a market full of all sorts of businesses, domestic and foreign, China has corporate horror stories to parallel those of other markets, and there is no shortage of material. The plots may vary, but each risk has its own themes and associated clichés—knowledge of which can help managers avoid falling into the same rusty old traps that "old China hands" may be able to spot a mile off (and even they need to be wary of new traps being placed in their path). But China business is not all bad, and some context is needed (see Table 1.1):

- The World Bank's 2014 Ease of Doing Business rakings[3] puts China at 96 out of 189 economies (up from 99 in 2013). Hong Kong comes just behind Singapore, at number two, while Taiwan comes in at 16. The US sits in fourth position, Russia is the only one of the BRICS to come ahead of China, at 92, while Brazil is at 116, and India 132.

Table 1.1   BRICs business rankings

	Brazil	Russia	India	China
Corruption Perception Index '13 (Transparency International[4])	72	127	94	80
Ease of Business Rank '14 (World Bank[5])	116	92	132	96
Economic Freedom Rank '14 (Heritage Foundation[6])	114	140	120	137
Country Risk Assessment '14 (Coface[7])	A4	B	A4	A3
Trust Score '14 (Edelman[8])	N/A	38%	35%	36%

- The Heritage Foundation's 2014 Index of Economic Freedom[9] rankings (out of 178) has Hong Kong (as usual) ahead of Singapore at the top of the table, and Taiwan at 17. The US is at 12, Brazil 114, India 120, China 137, and Russia 140.

There is of course a lot of complexity within the rankings, and different risks will be relevant to different businesses. While the "ease of doing business" may sometimes seem to be a contradiction in terms, China is ranked alongside its BRICS peers, and is slowly rising up the global business rankings. There are of course still significant risk factors present in all these markets, and those most often discussed in the context of China business include:

- Bribery and corruption
- Fraud
- Intellectual property infringement
- Environment, health and safety

When it comes to topical, cross-border corporate risk issues, it is corruption that occupies front-of-mind for many. The AlixPartners 2014 Global Anti-Corruption Survey[10] (see Figure 1.1) found that 84 per cent of respondents noted "significant" (43 per cent) or "some" (41 per cent) risk of corruption in China, placing it more favorably overall than Brazil (86 per cent), and only just behind India (79 per cent) and Russia (81 per cent). While there are clearly significant risks, China is not an outlier on the scale.

Transparency International ranks China at 80 in its 2013 global Corruption Perceptions Index[11] (down from 39 in 2012), with Singapore at 5, Hong Kong at 15, and Taiwan at 36. Brazil was just above China at 72, with India following at 94, and Russia at 127.

It does not help that, in addition to perceived market risk, Chinese companies also face a credibility problem, with lack of trust in Chinese-headquartered companies remaining low, though on a par with Russia and India. According to Edelman[12] only 36 per cent of global respondents in the 2014 survey reported trust in Chinese companies, putting China between India (35 per cent) and Russia (38 per cent).

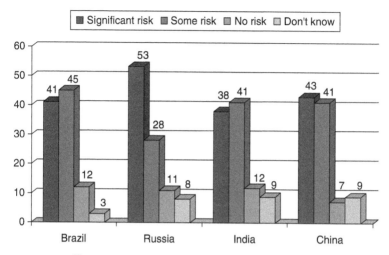

FIGURE 1.1 / 2014 Global Anti-Corruption Survey, AlixPartners; The BRICS (%)

Source: Data from AlixPartners Annual Global Anti-Corruption Survey, First Quarter, 2014: http://www.alixpartners.com/en/Publications/AllArticles/tabid/635/articleType/ArticleView/articleId/949/AlixPartners-Annual-Global-Anti-Corruption-Survey-Survey-of-General-Counsel-and-Compliance-Officers.aspx#sthash.7iN2dQB3.dpuf.

The low trust score may represent a heightened awareness of certain risks, or simply a lack of knowledge and engagement. Either way the result is that some international firms are losing out on opportunities in China, and that increasingly outward-looking Chinese firms are missing out on overseas investment opportunities—Edelman found that just 34 per cent of developed-market respondents would trust a Chinese buyer of a firm in their country. International firms seeking to do business in China, and those that may be a target of Chinese investment in their home country, can benefit from the additional knowledge and confidence that due diligence brings. As we will see later in the book, the due diligence process itself can be a tool for trust building.

Risky business in China is not just about China. It is also about processes and people. Just like anywhere else. But more so.

Risky Business in Brief: China Risk in Context

- *Business crime happens everywhere, but risk management requires adaptation*
- *China business risk is on a par with the BRICs ... but China is not optional*
- *Compliance with Chinese and FCPA/Bribery laws need to be embedded*
- *Internal and external fraud and corruption require attention*
- *Low levels of trust can be addressed with positive and proactive due diligence*

chapter 2

How Risky Is Business in China?

China challenges

There are many challenges that might keep China-focused mangers awake at night. Some of them, like the (lack of) quality of Beijing's air, they can do little about. Others are the subject of much debate, planning and effort. It is helpful to map out the range of concerns, and to put the key risks in the context of wider business issues.

China business news, and word-of-mouth reporting, suggests that market conditions continue to change quickly—as they always seem to have done. But a number of themes are consistently raised. These relate to issues such as rising costs, intellectual property rights (IPR) protection, market access, regulation, and competition. Surveys of the China business environment tend to suggest similar challenges. The US–China Business Council (USCBC), the American Chamber of Commerce in China (AmCham), and the European Chamber of Commerce in China (EUCCC), each produce an annual survey on the business environment, based on feedback from their membership. The key reported risks and challenges reported by the US and the European companies in China in 2013 are outlined in Table 2.1.

The business challenges cover a range of economic, political, legal, operational, and cultural issues. It is clear that costs are increasing across the board. The competition for qualified management and staff has also

Table 2.1 Challenges of foreign companies in China

Risk Themes 2013	US–China Business Council (Concerns)[1]	American Chamber of Commerce (Risks/ Challenges)[2]	EU Chamber of Commerce[3] (Challenges)
Costs	#1 Cost increases	#1 Rising labor costs (#1 challenge)	#1 Rising labor costs
Economic Growth	N/A	#2 Chinese economic slowdown #6 Global economic slowdown	#2 Chinese economic slowdown #3 Global economic slowdown
Competition	#2 Competition from Chinese companies	N/A	#5 Competition from private enterprises #9 Competition from State enterprises
Human Resources	#4 HR recruitment & retention	#3 Shortage of qualified employees (#3 challenge) #4 Shortage of qualified managers (#5 challenge)	#7 Lack of sufficient & qualified talent
Protectionism	#7 Non discrimination/ National treatment #10 Foreign investment restrictions	#5 Increased Chinese protectionism	#4 Market access barriers
Legal issues & enforcement	#3 Administrative Licensing	Inconsistent regulatory interpretation/ Unclear laws (#2 risk)	#6 Discretionary enforcement of regulations
	#5 IPR enforcement #6 Uneven enforcement of laws #9 Standards & conformity assessment	Obtaining required licenses (#6 challenge) Corruption (#4 challenge)	#10 Unlawful transactions
Other	#8 Transparency	#7 Deterioration of Sino-US relations	#8 RMB appreciation

intensified, and is one of the factors making rising costs the top concern overall. The fact that this is happening in an environment of slowing growth in China and around the world only compounds the problem, and it is therefore hardly surprising to see that competition is becoming more intense from private companies as well as Chinese state-owned enterprises (SOEs). Or that perceived protectionist measures that hamper foreign firms' ability to compete on a level playing field are worsening—ranging from access to finance and taxation benefits, to business licensing and project approvals.

Legal issues are another common cause for concern, and range from IPR and licensing problems to the uncertainty and commercial risk presented by inconsistent enforcement. In terms of IPR protection, 98 per cent of USCBC respondents noted it remained a concern, though they also reported that enforcement through the courts is slowly improving. Seventy-two per cent of AmCham's respondents indicated that China's IPR enforcement regime was either ineffective or totally ineffective. Not reassuring numbers for those with IP to protect. Other issues include changing bilateral relationships (which have commercial as well as political ramifications), corruption, and the longstanding debate over the value of the Chinese currency, the Renminbi (RMB).

As China is such an important market for international companies the challenges are ones that need to be addressed. The 2013 European Chamber Business Confidence Survey[4] summed it up well:

> Despite many of the lowest business confidence results since the onset of the global economic downturn, it is clear that China is still being perceived as the best of a challenging global situation. China continues to be a priority in global strategies and a mainstay for global revenue generation. European companies are resigning themselves to this reality and remain committed to the Chinese market:

> • China is seen as increasingly important in global strategies by 64 per cent of companies, albeit a decline from 74 per cent in 2012. China is rated as a top three country for future investments by 43% of companies.

- Further expansions to current China operations are considered by 86% of European companies.

Going forward, respondents are overwhelmingly united in their view of the key drivers for China's future economic performance:

- Rule of law and transparent policy-making was identified as a significant key driver by 76 per cent of companies.
- The promotion of fairer competition and fewer monopolies was also regarded to be a potentially significant driver of China's future economic performance by 68 per cent of companies.

The rule-of-law concerns are strategic in nature, but also relate to the real risks associated with crime. The "most significant white-collar crimes of 2013" of "more than 1,498,000 money-related crimes" that were investigated by Chinese police (as reported by *China Daily*[5]), included a range of globally recognizable risks:

- Frauds in the financial sector, and in relation to a major pyramid scheme
- Counterfeiting of drugs, tax invoices, money and bank cards
- Bribery in the pharmaceuticals sector
- Embezzlement by an insurance company executive
- Illegal foreign exchange trading
- Insider trading at a financial institution

The big cases that make it into *China Daily* only represent the tip of the iceberg, and the underlying risks, including the role of government and state-owned enterprises in business, are things that increasingly concern managers. Wang Yong, a professor at the China University of Political Science and Law in Beijing, wrote in the Chinese business publication, *Caixin*, that some parts of the private sector are almost forced into crime as a result of structural pressures[6]:

> Business crime issues are receiving considerable attention in China these days, and two crimes with Chinese "characteristics" distinctly stand out. One type of crime involves collusion between business and government officials. Another could be called the private sector's "crime of necessity."

Kroll's 2013–2014 Global Fraud Report presented a similar level of fraud risk in China to that noted in the AlixPartners corruption report referred to earlier. It also pointed to a significant negative change in sentiment[7]:

> The proportion of those reporting an increase in fraud exposure at their firms has grown from 69% in the 2012 survey to 80% this time. Moreover the sense of vulnerability in China towards conflicts of interest, vendor or procurement fraud, IP theft and regulatory or compliance breach has grown dramatically.

Kroll found that 67 per cent of respondent companies were affected by fraud in China, and that this most often arises from:

- Theft of assets or stock (23%)
- Management conflicts of interest (20%)
- Vendor, supplier, or procurement fraud (18%)
- Regulatory or compliance breach (15%)
- IP theft (15%)

The report also points to increased risk, with the average reported loss amounting to 1.2 per cent of revenue (up from 0.8 per cent from a year earlier). Despite the significant impact on revenues, there is surprisingly little impact on boardroom behavior, according to research from Ernst & Young. Their 12th Global Fraud Survey[8] reported that 93 per cent of respondents in China felt that their boards needed "a more detailed understanding of the business if it is to be an effective safeguard against fraud, bribery and corrupt practices." Globally the figure was 52 per cent, but the increased risk associated with markets like China was emphasized:

> In particular, respondents in rapid-growth markets see board understanding as being in need of development. This is a worrying development as many commentators argue that it is precisely these markets that pose the highest fraud, bribery and corruption risks.

With similar—high and increasing—levels of concern reported by the American Chamber of Commerce and Control Risks (see box below), investment in some preventative due diligence and risk management would seem to be sensible.

Current sentiment in China business is that "risk is as high as it has ever been," says Paul Gillis, author of the China Accounting Blog,[9] former PwC accountant, and current Professor at Guanghua School of Management at Peking University. He notes the financial frauds by Chinese companies have been exposed with the assistance of their US listings and the scrutiny of short sellers, but also that many other similar frauds certainly exist in the market.

According to Chris Cheung, Director of the EU SME[10] Centre in Beijing, there has been a significant increase in demand for advice on risk issues in China over the past few years, especially with regard to fraudulent behavior. More victims of fraud have been actively seeking assistance after suffering a loss and, perhaps as a result of higher risk-awareness, more client companies have been demanding preliminary due diligence on prospective partners and suppliers, especially since mid-2011. Typical cases involve European traders who order products having had little contact with the supplier, and often without ever visiting China, who find that their containers are empty or filled with substandard goods. In some cases the initial orders may be fine, but the quality drops off with subsequent shipments. Sometimes it seems to be a bait-and-switch tactic on the side of the suppliers, or it may simply be down to a lack of communication and understanding. Sadly the traders have no real recourse, because either the cost of going after the suppliers is too high in relation to the cost of goods ordered (often under Euros 20,000) or, when the losses are higher, because identification of the supplier and/or collection of evidence is difficult, according to Ludmila Hyklova, the Centre's Legal Advisor.[11]

Kent Kedl, Managing Director, Greater China and North Asia for Control Risks,[12] notes that 10–15 years ago the big foreign investors were rushing into China and staking out claims in a Wild West style. These days growth is much more organic, as the market is more developed, and as there is less money around. There is also less margin in many cases, so foreign investors have been looking for efficiencies, and opening the lid on their China operations. Some of them, according to Kedl, are finding surprises popping out, including fraudulent and corrupt ones. He suggests it is this voyage of discovery, and the increased awareness it brings, that gives the impression the risks are getting worse. In fact they have always been present but had previously been considered normal business practice or were just ignored by many.

SPECIALIST SPOTLIGHT: FRAUD & CORRUPTION

Kent Kedl, Control Risks[13]

Corruption/fraud continued to be ranked amongst the top five most serious business challenges for American companies operating in China, according to the "China Business Report 2012–2013" jointly released by Control Risks, a global business risk consultancy, and the American Chamber of Commerce in Shanghai (AmCham Shanghai) ...

Sixty-nine per cent of respondents indicated that corruption and fraud are a hindrance to their business, an increase of 8 per cent from last year. An overwhelming majority of companies (90 per cent) cited that the issue of corruption and fraud has either remain unchanged or has worsened, up from 84 per cent a year ago. The most common types of corruption reported were sales kickbacks to customers (58 per cent), followed by employee fraud (50 per cent) and government tenders (34 per cent).

The picture painted may be fairly gloomy, but it is less so than elsewhere, and most remain focused on the light at the end of the tunnel. China presents more potential for growth, even if it is as a slower (but more sustainable) pace than in recent years. Companies can certainly not ignore the opportunity, either as a manufacturing base or as an emerging consumer market.

On the manufacturing side there has been concern that China is no longer a low-cost market, due to rising wages, compliance and other costs, and over the past few years some companies such as General

Electric have made some moves to "re-shore" manufacturing (or aspects of it) away from China. Others have chosen to dilute their China exposure by developing a "China plus one" strategy, with some production being moved to low-cost bases such as Vietnam and Bangladesh.

There may be risks to avoid in, and cost savings to be made outside, China—but the risks tend to follow businesses wherever they go (Vietnam and Bangladesh have their own, well-reported problems). And the lure of the still-developing domestic Chinese market, combined with established supply-chain clusters and a very well-developed logistics infrastructure, means that, for most, China sourcing and/or sales are a necessity that is here to stay. This reality is reflected in the figures and, according to the World Trade Organization (WTO), China was the largest trader of goods in the world in 2013,[14] with a total of US$4.16 trillion (exports of US$2.21 trillion dollars and imports of US$1.95 trillion dollars). It is also the largest trading partner of 120 countries and regions, and for those that are most tightly bound to China's economy through trade and investment links, the risk increases with the degree of integration.[15] As a result, risks in China may be even more important to manage that in other markets in which the same risks are present.

While there are significant China challenges that some businesses would prefer to avoid altogether, the overall perception is that the potential rewards outweigh the risks. And that is likely to be true—at least for those companies that take an objective view of those risks, and proactive measures to mitigate them. For those that would prefer to ignore the potential for downside losses (and the benefits of a bit of due diligence) in favor of the more uplifting focus on market share, profits, and glory, there are no lack of cautionary tales to read before bedtime.

Risky Business in Brief: China Challenges

- *Rising costs and a slowing economy are impacting the operational environment*
- *Risks come from political, economic, legal, operational, and cultural issues*

- *Fraud, corruption, and intellectual property risks are core concerns*
- *Perceived risks are increasing for foreign companies in China*
- *SMEs and new sectors are engaging China but lack awareness of risk issues*

Risks "with Chinese characteristics"

Due diligence is an important element in balancing business risk anywhere. It is especially essential when the weight of risk factors increase due to exposure to new markets, new people, and new sectors. In a market like China, which operates a socialist market economy "with Chinese characteristics," there often needs to be a pause for thought and recalibration. Critical information can be opaque or completely obscured, and different definitions, cultural norms, and business benchmarks may make it difficult for the uninitiated to successfully transfer their usual confidence in judging people and situations. As onetime China media entrepreneur, and *China Cuckoo* author, Mark Kitto[16] puts it:

> It is tough doing business in China. Not only for foreigners. Chinese entrepreneurs go through the same hell by a different route. But if you are a foreigner you are at a disadvantage from the start, not only because of who you are but also because you think like a foreigner and always will, no matter how hard you try to adapt.

In addition to globally present risks such as fraud, bribery, and corruption (which need no explanation here, but which will be covered later on), there are some features of Chinese cultural, economic, and business life that can create confusion and increase risk for the uninitiated, and which require the re-focusing of the average pair of Western reading glasses if they are to be seen clearly. When they are misread, or completely ignored (as is still all-too-often the case) by foreigners trying to do business (or plan or evaluate due diligence) in China, there can be negative consequences. Some of the notable Chinese characteristics which might jump off the page and give the unsuspecting business reader a nasty surprise (or a handy insight), include:

- Guanxi networks
- Giving and losing face
- Political rule of law
- Differences and disparities
- Information informatization
- Different dreams and mutual benefits
- Legal representatives, chops, and phantoms
- Shadow banking
- Fake receipts
- Variable interest entities (VIEs)

Guanxi networks

"Guanxi," or relationships, can be hard to understand and complex to navigate. So much that is said about guanxi is clichéd—and so much of it is true, especially the bits about it being complicated and important!

What is clear is that there is a cultural divide in terms of the Chinese and Western approaches to doing business, and to developing and using guanxi. To a visiting foreigner, some dinners, stories, and a few days spent discussing business may seem like guanxi-building. But the foreigner's focus is usually on doing business first, and developing the long-term relationship over the course of the business dealings. A Chinese counterpart may be more focused on first establishing that the foreigner can be trusted before venturing into business. Katherine Peavy of Cross Pacific Partner[17] has worked in an advisory role at a risk management company in Shanghai, and as a supply chain risk manager for a major international business in China. Her view is that "foreigners don't have guanxi," partly because Chinese counterparts expect they will eventually leave (most do), so are not long-term propositions.

Andrew Hupert, author of *Guanxi for the Busy American*[18] has pointed out that Chinese business people have always used guanxi as part of their natural due diligence process. Their contacts are used to provide introductions to the right people, themselves trusted members of the wider network. The risk of damaging a business partner from the network includes a risk of damaging a long chain of valued relationships, so protections are built in. Hupert also emphasizes that in China guanxi does not rest. Like a plant that needs regular watering, it needs constant attention and cannot be abandoned after that one, week-long business trip. Investing time in building and maintaining these Chinese (personal) business relationships is every bit as important to a foreign business person as investing money in paying the phone bill every month. If the investment stops, the line may go dead.

For a Chinese person, with deep roots in a relationship, continual care is still required. The case of a Chinese businessman helps illustrate how the mechanics of guanxi can work. His family was very prominent in mainland China, and he was successful in business. He had excellent guanxi in political and business fields at the highest levels, as well as an ability to unravel complex issues, and help solve otherwise intractable problems for his network. The guanxi may have seemed inherited or effortlessly developed from the outside, but it was built on generations of family connections, and maintained with the help of a large database, a dedicated staff, a sense of humor, and a busy role as a generous host and a valued advisor and business matchmaker. Like a complex machine, guanxi needs regular oiling and attention.

Real Guanxi runs deep, and flows in two directions. It cannot be bought, and cannot be built overnight—but it can last a long time, and prove invaluable at a time of need. A long history, combined with thoughtful, regular activity is ideal—but even for those that can't manage the history quite yet, attentiveness and thoughtfulness in personal relationships are essential. As credit insurance company Coface noted in relation to payment default risk in their 2013 China survey[19]:

> the respondents have indicated what the most effective actions are in case of non-payment. "Amicable negotiation on repayment schedule," according to the 82% of the respondents, is the most effective action in such cases. We assume that the importance of guanxi

(relationship) in Chinese business culture could be a major reason of such findings, as Chinese business practitioners tend to believe that "all problems can be solved with good relationships."

While a business may be able to benefit commercially from developing strong relationships with officials in high places, or by hiring the friends and relatives of such people, they can also come unstuck when those people move on, or when compliance catches up with them. It is obviously necessary to develop personal and corporate connections in China, but it is also necessary to develop them with an eye on legal compliance, and to make sure those relationships are sustainable through strategic alignment of interests rather than simply through the employment of relatives or giving of gifts.

Giving and receiving face

The Chinese concept of face ("mianzi") is not alien to non-Chinese, but it is one that is central to Chinese cultural sensitivities, and deserving of special attention. It also presents the unwary foreign business person with a real risk.

The giving, losing, gaining, and saving of face in China goes well beyond a desire to flatter, or to avoid being embarrassed. It has deep cultural roots, and practical application in everyday business and personal life, and daily conversation. Some things that might be considered time-saving and professional in a New York state of mind may be considered social death in a Beijing office block. Polished, successful MBA-types who wade into a Chinese business environment full of frank, honest opinions may find out the hard way that a lack of cultural sugar-coating can fast bring on another Chinese cultural experience—eating bitter ("chi ku"). Bitter is how a co-panellist at a conference felt when lost face lost him a Euros 2.5 million real estate deal. A group (another Chinese characteristic) of five prospective clients were on site to sign the contracts and buy properties that would secure them investment visas in Portugal. However, they suddenly got up, left, and bought similar properties from a competitor the next day. The reason was later explained. Nobody from the seller's management team had thought to attend the contract signing, and the investors felt uncomfortable with the deal due to loss of face.

Hierarchy is also important in China, and has its roots in Confucianism. Youngsters should respectfully defer to elders, employees to bosses, and students to teachers. In the business context this means that Chinese employees are generally reticent to stand up publicly to a more senior person in an organization, or even to point out an error that could result in loss of face. For someone who wants to gather potentially sensitive information this can result in a need for more, and more subtle, forms of communication. For someone who takes a lack of negativity at face value, and misses the strong currents that flow below the surface, it can result in a need for damage limitation later on.

Face can be a difficult concept for foreigners in China, and a balance needs to be struck between a soft and flattering approach and polite but firm requests for information and explanations. It is important to understand the cultural background and to recognize that while it can be a useful oil for the works, the pressures of face can also make communicating bad news difficult in either direction. It is therefore a good idea to tune an ear to the subtleties of Chinese speech ("I understand" may not mean "I agree," and "OK" may not mean that everything is!).

Giving of face is often linked with the giving of gifts and the hosting of banquets, and this has long been part and parcel of Chinese business life. Not all gifts are equal of course, and there is a dividing line somewhere between the traditional piece of local craftwork or corporate pen, and the vintage bottles of booze and gold-plated books which have occasionally made the news. The latter would certainly risk crashing into a wall of compliance and accusations of bribery.

SPECIALIST SPOTLIGHT: FACE VALUE IN CHINESE SOCIETY

Guy Olivier Faure, China Europe International Business School[20]

Face saving, face restoration, and face giving are crucial values. The Chinese live in the eyes of the others and have a quasi-pathological preoccupation with reputation. Social judgment as a personal asset and as a family asset is considered as vital. The worst thing that can happen to the Chinese is to lose face, to feel humiliated.

This explains a number of situations that make the Westerners in China somehow puzzled. For instance, not showing ignorance is more important than telling the truth. Maintaining face has priority over the accuracy of the answer. In relations between foreign and Chinese enterprises, face concerns lead to references to "technical cooperation" instead of "technical assistance." A foreign businessperson has to realize that one does not sell to China, but it is China that buys.

The regulating mechanism of social behavior is the feeling of shame instilled in the mind of every Chinese. Face may not only be enhanced or lost but also "traded" by giving face to the counterpart who in turn has to reciprocate.

Face has also a negative value because it serves as an "invisible knife"[21] to kill genuine feelings. Without a sharp sense of shame, China with its lost legal framework and weak sense of discipline would have been a disorganized society deprived of social cohesion. In this sense, face is a founder value of social order.

Indirect action is a tribute to Confucius, a way to preserve harmony. The whole society should be the replication of a large family. Social harmony is achieved through moral conduct, controlling emotions, avoiding conflict, even competition. Thus, in relationships things are suggested, not told straight away.

Westerners in China tend sometimes to think that what their Chinese counterparts practice the best is the art of dodging. This is not to be seen as a trick to deceive foreigners but an immediate product of the doctrine of harmony and the face consciousness. The point is to prevent a polarization of positions that could result in a conflicting situation. Consequently divergences in interests are not openly stated, leaving a rather opaque situation in which the foreign counterparts exhaust themselves while trying to understand what is really going on. The Westerner may thus realize that the Chinese discourse is meaningful for what it does not tell.

Political rule of law

Political leaders in the West are often lawyers (think Obama, Clinton, Blair), and the law is what makes the Western world go round. Political leaders in China are Party (that is, Communist Party) people, and it is powerful people who make things happen in China, within China's own legal framework.

Political issues are not unique to China, but various levels of government, and especially the Communist Party of China (CPC),[22] play a very important role in economic policy, state-owned enterprises, and business activities generally, and they require sensitive handling. The central government, and local government, should always be considered as stakeholders and, as such, should be covered as part of any stakeholder mapping and risk analysis. Equally, central government policies tend to set clearly defined directions for the wind to blow in. It makes sense to align with, not run against, such powerful forces.

In some cases, for example where a project may touch on sensitive national or local issues, such as employment, the environment or health and safety, special care and attention should be given to the resulting risks, even if they are not strictly part of the commercial terms of reference. The example, from 1993, of Rupert Murdoch proclaiming that his Hong Kong-based Star (satellite) TV network would help hasten the development democracy was not well received by China's leadership[23] — but has been a great case study. Unsurprisingly, he was not made welcome, and spent many years trying to resurrect the relationship. Had he been more attuned to the political risk, he may have had a much easier ride. In other cases, it may be that a project relies directly or indirectly on the support of a key government department or official. What is the risk to the project if the relevant official moves on (or is removed without notice)? Should a lack of a broad base of support among relevant officials be identified as a risk factor, a refined government communications plan might need to be developed as mitigation.

The risk of officials, or senior executives in state-owned enterprises, being suddenly removed is not an academic one. It happened with great drama in the municipality of Chongqing, with the downfall of its previously powerful Party Secretary, Bo Xilai. The impact on local development projects was also dramatic, as local government posts were quickly reshuffled, priorities reset, and projects pushed back. In the high-profile, multi-billion dollar development of high-speed rail in China, things went off the rails after a number of accidents, and the former Minister, Liu Zhijun, was removed from his position and then charged with corruption, embezzlement, and abuse of power.[24] Any company planning to use banks of guanxi, carefully built up with Liu and his ministry, to help them profit from China's railway boom would have had to suddenly re-think.

Only a rounded, strategic approach that is aligned with China's political and economic policies is likely to stand the test of time, and to get the support of new sets of officials trying to achieve China's development targets.

In terms of the role of the rule of law, Chinese regulations can be loosely drafted and left open to a degree of local interpretation and implementation by officials and courts (which are part of, not independent from, the state). Contracting parties in the West might take a conservative and legalistic approach to pre-emptive problem-solving—filling contracts with lots of penalty clauses and protections, on the assumption that operational issues are secondary and that, in the event of a problem, a third-party institution will make an independent decision on a case. In China things are less legalistic and more relationship-driven. It is therefore better to identify and avoid, or adapt to, the risks at an early stage, focusing on managing the relationship and dodging legal complications. While the Chinese courts and arbitration services have been developing rapidly, as any sport fan (or lawyer) will know, there is less chance of winning away from home.

Legal recourse alone is seldom enough to achieve a positive outcome in Chinese business disputes. It is not only important to plan around the legal risks but also to maintain the right relationships, stay abreast of local developments (via other channels than the counterparty), and react quickly when change is in the air.

Information informatization

Information can be confusing, especially when it is "informatized." China made its "informatization" plan in 2006, as has been officially noted:[25]

> The State Informatization Development Strategy (2006–2020) published by General Office of the CPC Central Committee and General Office of the State Council sets forth China's goals in informatization development for the next 15 years.

These top-down goals include strengthening the technical capability and capacity of the country's information infrastructure and industry, as well as "making effective progress on building more information-oriented national economy and society." Among the nine key aspects of the strategy is the aim of "exploiting information resources more efficiently." Information confusion and overload are common problems, and while there may be reams of data available, it may be inaccurate, out of date, or even fraudulent. It needs careful management, source and date confirmation, documentary verification, cross-checking, sense-checking, and objective analysis.

Different official data may be released by different departments, and even then it may be subject to later revisions. Data released by businesses may also not be perfect, especially if there are vested interests. On a macro level, GDP and trade data are frequently called into question (there is a even a sister book to this one—*Myth-Busting China's Numbers*, by Matthew Crabbe—which looks at the issue in detail). Crabbe[26] warns that "Chinese statistics need to be dealt with cautiously" and that they should not simply be taken at face value. Several sources should be consulted, disclaimers should be checked, and it should be noted if there are any significant omissions, as well as whether the nature of the data has changed over time. On a more positive note, Crabbe says that data is getting better with more accessible and online sources, and as the government's control over much of it is weakening.

Some of this is down to the sheer size and complexity of China, and the difficulty in collecting data. Some of it relates back to corporate reporting, and is another sign that companies might not always report the whole truth. On the release of China's surprisingly strong trade data for January 2014, *The Wall Street Journal*'s ChinaRealTime report noted[27]:

> Export growth of 10.6% on-year far outstripped forecasts of a 0.1% rise, while imports, up 10%, also came in way ahead of expectations … But analysts were quick to point out that China's trade data have been badly distorted in the past by exporters overstating the value of their shipments to bring money into the country illegally … So is global trade growth back on track? Or are companies fudging the numbers again?

Growth may well have been back on track, but companies were certainly sometimes fudging the numbers. This may be critical in terms of evaluating a set of accounts, but it can also have an impact when trying to assess things like market share as part of a commercial due diligence process. For example, a market researcher finding a piece of news about supply and demand in a certain industry may not want to take at face value the level of quoted investment, nor the targeted output. Clearly the news provider has a business interest in suggesting that the market will be well served by the investment (leaving, in theory, little opportunity for competitors), and in showing off to local officials how much money and employment will flow from their enlightened decision to approve the project. Cross-checking and, where possible, verification are needed if the figures are to hold any water.

Differences and disparities

China is a continental-sized country, with massive environmental, cultural, and economic differences between regions. There is no single way to look at China, and what is normal, or at least tolerated, in one part may be cracked down on in another. The Chinese saying that "heaven is high and the Emperor is far away" indicates that what might be allowed around the edges might not be appropriate under the noses of the leadership in Beijing. The government itself has used the concept to test new policies in the past. The first Special Economic Zone was established in 1980, in the southern city of Shenzhen, on the border with (the then British colony of) Hong Kong. Deng Xiaoping, the leader of the day, later used his famous 1992 "Southern Tour" to launch economic reforms with Shenzhen at their heart. It was no coincidence that the new President, Xi Jinping, made Shenzhen the destination of his first official visit—a barely coded message that he was serious about economic reform.

Building it. Not living it[28]

As well as differences in the application of policy and regulation, there are significant regional differences in development, infrastructure, income, and industry focus, as well as in spoken dialects, food, and style. Something that is a big investment in a second-tier city in Western China might be a big deal, but it would barely register on the radar in Shanghai. Compliance issues might be the major concern to officials in one city, while it might be employment or investment in another. Each place has its own priorities and constraints, and it is generally down to local officials to apply the national rules within the local context. This could make things seem easy for the big investor in the small town, who may find it simple to get things approved at the local level. While Beijing may be able to ignore the odd local idiosyncrasy, there are red lines that should not be crossed, and improperly approved projects that are at odds with key national interests (e.g., in relation to environmental protection or tax reliefs) are not likely to escape review for long. The documentation may seem to be in order, and the Mayor may be at the banquet, but the risk may lie at a higher level.

Wealth disparity is another big political and social issue for China, and it also impacts on business risk. International investments and contracts with multinational companies involve large amounts of money anywhere, but in an environment with relatively low wages, under a system that is driven by people in positions of political power (and where "to get rich is glorious"), bribery and corruption may flourish if unchecked.

It is common knowledge that there is a kickback culture in procurement, with some sectors being especially bad. As noted earlier, 67 per cent of companies surveyed by Kroll in China reported they were affected by fraud. It is common sense that more money on the table will result in more risk, and that compliance and risk management systems which may work well in a more wealthy, legalistic, and developed market may not work everywhere. Assumptions should be questioned and systems adapted to suit the risks faced on the ground in China—whichever part of China that may be.

Different dreams and mutual benefits

Many of the troubled joint-venture stories of the early and mid-1990s were diagnosed as suffering from "different dreams" syndrome. This sickness was apparent even in the early, classic text on Western investment in China, *Beijing Jeep*,[29] in which Jim Mann wrote that:

> The ultimate question was whether two partners with such different dreams could last for long in the same bed.

The same bed/different dreams concept became something of a cliché, but it made a good point well. There is a major risk of misunderstanding between Chinese and foreign business people, and this is driven by differing approaches to life, business, and everything ... even when both sides start the relationship by raising small glasses of strong liquor and toasting to "mutual benefit"—a phrase that frequently punctuates Chinese business discussions, and a concept that may last no longer than the swiftly downed drink.

The foreigner often rushes in, eager to make a profitable, legally watertight deal in an exciting market, and then return home to the family, job done. Over time a relationship can develop with the Chinese partners, and that would be great. The chances are someone else will be responsible for the implementation and operations anyway. "Let's agree the details and get the contract signed!" The Chinese counterpart also wants to make a profit, but first wants to assess the foreign partner before deciding what can be done in terms of business. The risks and benefits at home are long term, both to the business and the personal network. Even a short-term loss might mean a good long-term deal, if the business can be won, and a profit made over time. "Let's get to know each other (with the help of some baijiu[30] and karaoke), and we'll work out any issues as they arise."

The problem is that, with different starting points, the travelling partners begin to diverge right from the beginning, so that when problems do need to be addressed there is already a gulf between them. As Andrew Hupert puts it in *The Fragile Bridge: Conflict Management in Chinese Business*[31]: "set expectations early on by making business philosophy, standards and limits clear as part of the introductory conversations." If the focus of the foreigner is simply on getting the lowest cost or the fastest turnaround, then the Chinese side will reasonably see those as the drivers. Call up in six months and complain about the quality, demand in-process inspections, or health and safety audits at the factory, and expect an unfriendly response from a partner who may feel betrayed, and whose own personal relationships may be put at risk.

There may be more than one dream[32]

Legal representatives, chops, and phantoms

The person with legal authority in a Chinese company, the "legal representative," needs to be identified in order to help avoid frauds, and to ensure that negotiations are carried out with somebody who actually has contractual authority. Due diligence to confirm the identity of a Chinese company's legal representative can be achieved by checking the company's business license, or the corporate records held by the local office of the Administration of Industry & Commerce (AIC).

Chops, which are used as company seals on official documents, are as important as a valid signature on a Western contract, and should be registered with the Public Security Bureau (PSB). In China, a chop can commit a company to a contract. As a result the company chop needs to be guarded with care by the owner, and watched with care by any stakeholders.

Phantom shareholders, or beneficial/controlling owners, may not be those listed on a company's official filings. Sometimes, for a variety of reasons, the real owners hide behind a front, who may be a family member, friend, or associate. It is important to know the truth in order to avoid conflicts of interest and political risks. It is not only the shareholders who may be phantom, and only due diligence can confirm whether a target company is really a registered, legal, and operational entity; a proper company, but only a shadow of the one described; a shell set up only for the purposes of committing a fraud; or simply a phantom company, intent on giving the less diligent of potential partners an expensive nightmare.

SPECIALIST SPOTLIGHT: LEGAL REPRESENTATIVES IN CHINA

Liu Xiangwen, Xia Dongxia and Li Xiny, King & Wood Mallesons[33]

Under PRC laws, the legal representative of a company is the person who acts in the name of the company and represents the company in the exercise of its rights and obligations. The legal representative is a fundamental part of a company's corporate governance structure. To an extent, the person who is appointed to the position of the legal representative is authorized to conduct many of the company's affairs. However, the legal representative must fulfil certain duties while exercising his/her rights.

According to this provision, a company's legal representative must meet two conditions: she/he must: (a) be the core management personnel of the company, i.e. the chairman of the board, the general manager or executive director of the company; and (b) complete the formalities for application or amendment of business registration.

Generally speaking, when a legal representative acts in accordance with the laws, administrative regulations, and articles of association of a company, such acts shall be deemed acts of the company and the liability arising out of such activities are assumed by the company.

Shadow banking

In the 1990s the debt problems in the news from China were "triangular" debt and non-performing loans (NPLs), and an international bond payment default by Guangdong International Trust & Investment Corp. (GITIC) in 1998.[34] The original non-performing loans may have been successfully wrapped up into specially formed asset management companies (AMCs), but fast forward to 2014, and the debt stories are still blowing up. *The Wall Street Journal* reported in February 2014[35]:

> Driven by a surge in borrowing in recent years, Chinese companies amassed an estimated $12.1 trillion of debt at the end of last year, according to Standard & Poor's. That compares with an estimated $12.9 trillion for U.S. businesses, now the world's most indebted. The ratings company estimates that debt at Chinese companies is poised to exceed the U.S. total this year or next.

> According to J.P. Morgan Chase … China's corporate debt was 124% of gross domestic product in 2012, up from 111% in 2010 and 92% in 2008. J.P. Morgan economist Haibin Zhu said the number likely rose further in 2013.

> Corporate debt in comparable emerging economies is 40% to 70% of GDP, while in the U.S. the figure is 81%, according to J.P. Morgan.

There is significant off-balance sheet lending in some already challenged sectors (such as coal mining, which has suffered from over-capacity).

Much of the shadow banking business is managed by Trust companies, who often work together with mainstream banks to market their products. The China Trustee Association has reported[36] that Chinese Trusts had as much as RMB10.9 trillion (US$1.8 billion) under the management at the end of 2013. In February 2014, Reuters reported on the fragility of the situation, referencing a high-profile case[37]:

> A high-yield investment product backed by a loan to a debt-ridden coal company failed to repay investors when it matured … in the latest sign of financial stress in China's shadow bank sector. The product, which raised 289 million yuan ($47.7 million) from wealthy clients of China Construction Bank (CCB), China's second-largest lender, was created by Jilin Province Trust Co Ltd and backed by a loan to a coal company, Shanxi Liansheng Energy Co Ltd. … Analysts warn that default risk from such off-balance-sheet loans is rising. Funds raised through the sale of these products typically flow to weak borrowers that struggle to access bank loans, especially property developers, local governments and firms in industries plagued by overcapacity.

By March, the situation had worsened, and Shanghai Chaori Solar Energy Science missed an interest payment deadline on its corporate bonds,[38] and became the first Chinese company to default. A rapid reassessment of risks followed, and may yet result in a more balanced approach in the long term.

From a due diligence perspective, even if loans or debts are properly recorded on a company's books, the risks associated with them might not be obvious. Therefore a closer look may be needed, starting with the context of the business sector—real estate and mining, for example, as well as any of those high-energy consuming, high-polluting industries that have gone out of political fashion, would already represent big red flags.

Fake receipts

Fake receipts "fapiaos" are big business in China, and are central to many financial frauds. In 2013 Chinese officials reportedly[39] seized 130 million forged official receipts, investigated 91,000 cases, arrested 9,799 people, punished 89,000 enterprises, and investigated fake receipts worth RMB88 billion. The chances of coming across faked fapiaos in the course of financial due diligence or when dealing with expenses claims are high.

Weng Yee Ng of Forensic Risk Alliance (FRA),[40] a forensic accounting and risk consultancy, explains that, the government endorses the use of a fapiao which is an official receipt that can serve as final proof-of-purchase of goods and services. However, in an effort to reduce taxes paid, some individuals purchase fapiaos from different vendors at a fraction of their face value, obscuring their true cost of purchasing goods and services. In some instances, an individual can obtain false fapiaos for the cost of about one per cent of the total receipt amount.

Variable interest entities

The variable interest entity (VIE) structure has had a lot of attention in China since around 2000, as it has been an important element in a number of corporate frauds, and as it lives in a somewhat grey area of the law. The structure provides a contractual mechanism that allows a foreign party to invest indirectly in areas of the economy that are highly regulated, and which may restrict direct foreign investment. Since 2011, when there was a high-profile VIE case[41] involving Alibaba's transfer of its Alipay online payments arm to a company controlled by Jack Ma, Alibaba's founder, there has been increased scrutiny of the structure, both in China and overseas. According to a Bloomberg article in December 2013[42]:

> The scrutiny follows some little noticed legal developments in China over the past 18 months that show the contracts behind the foreign listings may not hold up in court ... The U.S. Securities and Exchange Commission has pressed Beijing-based Baidu Inc. (BIDU), China's No. 1 search engine, to make additional disclosures about its corporate structure, citing the potential for foreign owners to lose control.
>
> Separately, the Hong Kong Stock Exchange added a requirement ... for companies that seek to list using the structure to obtain a legal

opinion stating that their contracts don't break rules or laws, and won't be invalidated.

The article also notes that in August 2012 the Chinese Ministry of Commerce barred Wal-Mart from taking control of the value-added telecommunications services of Yihoadian, an online retailer, using a VIE structure. Then, in October 2012, China's Supreme Court invalidated a similar contract that aimed to give a foreign company (Hong Kong's Chinachem Financial Services) control over China's Minsheng Banking Corporation, on the basis that the structure was "concealing illegal intentions with a lawful form." Telecommunications and banking services have always been sensitive and restricted areas for foreign investors in China, so it seems that tacit acceptance of the VIE structure will only go so far, and that investors need to understand the risks and limitations of the model. Paul Gillis notes on his China Accounting Blog[43]:

> The variable interest entity (VIE) structure, where companies are controlled with contracts is a common enabler of ... scams. Shareholders have little, if any, legal protection when things go wrong with a VIE.

Risky Business in Brief: Risks with Chinese Characteristics

- *They may be clichéd, but "Chinese characteristics" create risk if ignored*
- *Political rule of law requires focus on people and policy, not just legal issues*
- *Cultural issues such as face and guanxi have a business and risk impact*
- *Different dreams for two parties usually results in sleepless nights for one*
- *Some things are just different (chops, fapiaos, shadow lending and VIEs)*

Bad news is news

The sections above have outlined some of the local challenges faced by foreign business in China, as well as some of the risks … "with Chinese characteristics." It is easy to see these risks in black and white on paper, turn the page, and move swiftly on. But in reality, even seasoned executives at large, well-established foreign companies do occasionally get caught out. They sometimes also get called out in the world business news. There's no news like bad news, but the only way for good to come of it is to learn the lessons, and avoid falling into the same traps.

Risk has always been topical in China, but it is especially relevant now given recent news stories that have highlighted corporate bribery, fraud, and investment losses, as well as a crackdown on investigators, and restrictions on access to corporate records. For example, in the recent past China watchers have had a full range of risk-awareness materials served up on the news. A few of the bigger cases are outlined below, highlighting some common problems, including:

- Accounting fraud
- Bribery
- Personal data abuses
- Supply chain contamination
- Faked qualifications
- Trademark litigation
- Commercial disputes

Importantly, while the stories were all "news," none of the issues were new to the market (or even to some of the protagonists), but they all helped to fuel the fear that managers feel about the risks of doing business in China. They are a valuable part of the China risk story, but they are only one side of it. All of them resulted in large part from a lack of due diligence and internal controls, and a lack of awareness of how the environment was changing. No matter how big the company, how much or how long they have invested in China, how old their "China hands" are, or how clever the analysts, there is a risk that their assumptions can be overtaken by the rapid pace of change, or that a shift of policy focus can mean that previously unwatched areas fall foul of official scrutiny. The other, brighter, side of the story is that with structured, regular risk analysis, many of these problems can be avoided or controlled. But good news is not news.

Some recent, real-world examples of risk in action (and in the news) follow, and serve to highlight the need for sensible companies of all sizes and complexions operating in China to have robust risk identification and mitigation processes (not to mention crisis management plans) in place. The sooner the better.

Accounting for fraud

The US construction equipment company Caterpillar spent US$677 million on its purchase of the Chinese firm ERA Mining Machinery (the owner of Siwei Mechanical & Electrical Equipment Manufacturing Co Ltd., "Siwei"). A deal that was heralded as cross-border deal of the year when it was done in 2012.

But a year is a long time in business … and the deal soon unravelled, exposing fraudulent accounts, and a startling lack of due diligence for a deal that not only involved a lot of money, but which was also central to the company's strategy in one of the world's most important markets. According to a Reuters report,[44] Caterpillar discovered "deliberate, multi-year, coordinated accounting misconduct" at Siwei soon after the deal was completed. The *Reuters* investigation noted:

> Accounting problems were rampant at Siwei before Caterpillar bought it. Yet at multiple junctures, Caterpillar chose to ignore existing or potential problems and push ahead with the deal … it has become a case study in how a foreign company with decades of experience in China can still flounder in that market. It also shows how willing some multinationals are to accept risks they might otherwise avoid to establish themselves in the world's second-largest economy.

Bad news for Caterpillar, but not news in terms of financial fraud. The issue has long been chewed over, and the problems of US-listed Chinese companies had already made a significant market impact by 2012. Any investor with an interest in the performance of Chinese-listed companies would have found it hard not to notice. In July 2013 the *McKinsey Quarterly*[45] referenced the grand scale of the problem, and the financial impact that had already been demonstrated:

> It's not often that the credibility of an entire class of companies is called into question at once. The aggregate market capitalization of US-listed Chinese companies fell in 2011 and 2012 by 72 percent—and around one in five was delisted—even as the Nasdaq rose by 12 percent Nor is delisting of Chinese companies purely a US phenomenon: since 2008, around one in ten Chinese companies listed in Singapore has also been delisted or suspended.

It has long been widely accepted that company accounts in China should be taken with a pinch of salt, and a lot of investigation and sense-checking is needed in order to ensure that the content of the paperwork accurately reflects the operation of the business. McKinsey notes that fraud was often the issue in these cases, and that such things can be hard to identify, even with professional support:

> [They] often involved false or misleading documentation that would not have been discovered by a regular audit—since such audits primarily rely on documentation supplied by the company itself. Indeed, almost all the companies involved were audited by Big Four firms; most were brought to the market through IPO or reverse takeover by major US investment banks. Even investigative diligence, which can be extremely costly and time-consuming, has been far from foolproof; past examples have shown that private-equity and strategic investors can miss accounting fraud despite conducting a detailed, professional diligence.

The China Stock Fraud Blog[46] listed cases of reportedly fraudulent Chinese stocks in a 2013 post. Paul Gillis, in his China Accounting Blog noted that[47]:

> The author lists 121 companies; 54 in the US and Canada, 44 in Hong Kong, and 23 in Singapore. It is the best list I have seen

of Hong Kong and Singapore frauds. A number of alleged but unproven frauds are not included, even though some of these remain suspended from trading (i.e. AMBO, FU). The author lists no alleged frauds on Chinese exchanges.

The risks of reliance on box-ticking from the comfort of an air-conditioned office have been highlighted many times. And as McKinsey points out, it is unwise to rely entirely on documents supplied by the due diligence target (in China or anywhere else). While investigative diligence may not be foolproof, it need not be extremely costly, and it is certainly a sensible precaution. When properly deployed it can provide actionable intelligence and risk mitigation. And it could save the day.

The aptly named short-selling specialist Muddy Waters provided a number of examples of effective due diligence when focusing on financial frauds by US-listed Chinese companies back in 2011.[48] They managed to un-muddy the waters that had blinded all those professional IPO advisers, and saw through the frauds because, when they saw some red warning flags, they got out of the office, armed themselves with some research, and got down to the operating level to see for themselves the reality of the business (or the lack of it).

Bribery: bad for health

The Chinese pharmaceutical industry has long been considered corrupt, in part because of the way in which it is structured—with hospitals relying on income from the sale of drugs, and with doctors receiving very low pay. It was not a great surprise to people involved in the industry that bribes were being paid in order to get drugs into hospitals, and to boost drug company sales.

It was however a surprise to many when the blue-chip British multinational GSK made headlines as its executives were detained in China. The *Financial Times* reported[49] allegations that the company had used a network of some 700 travel agents to funnel RMB3 billion (US$500 million) in bribes to officials and doctors. GSK executives have paid a high personal price, and the business also suffered, with China sales reported to be down over 60% after the bribery allegations were made.

GSK was the first to be targeted in the anti-bribery campaign in the industry, but others, such as Sanofi, Novartis, Eli Lilly and Bayer, as well as some local companies, were also reported to be under scrutiny. And that was despite a seemingly robust approach to internal risk management. According to a Reuters report[50]:

> [D]espite conducting up to 20 internal audits in China a year, including an extensive 4-month probe earlier in 2013, GSK bosses were blindsided by police allegations of massive corruption involving travel agencies used to funnel bribes to doctors and officials.

Nonetheless, it was an obvious area for suspicion, according Paul Gillis, who noted[51]:

> Travel agencies are used like ATMs in China to distribute out illegal payments. Any company that does not have their internal audit department all over travel agency spending is negligent.

Additional coverage of the GSK case in the *Financial Times* pointed out that this sort of spending is commonplace, and that the annual reports of several listed Chinese showed that they[52]:

> paid out enormous sums in "sales expenses," including travel costs and fees for sales meetings, marketing "business development" and "other expenses."

It may be easy to blame the companies and the managers for lack of internal controls, or plain wrong-doing, but the risks in this case were not simply about commercial bribery. It was also about policy. The Chinese government has been promoting domestic consumption as a key economic policy, and one of the critical platforms for this change is reform of the healthcare system—building thousands of hospitals, and expanding to near universal healthcare coverage—so that more people will spend, rather than save as a hedge against illness. With such a large, and aging, population, China also needed to control healthcare costs, and thus the profits of the big pharmaceutical companies. Add to the policy mix President Xi Jinping's ongoing anti-corruption campaign, and the cosy relationship between big pharma, big hospitals, and some big officials, started to look distinctly uncomfortable. As it certainly did for a former director of the State Food and Drug Administration, Zheng Xiaoyu, who was executed in 2007 for corruption,[53] including receiving bribes from pharmaceutical companies. The risks were not exclusive to the pharmaceutical sector, and China-watchers may also recall the arrest of the "Rio Tinto Four" for bribery and theft of business secrets in 2009.[54] That case did act as a wake-up call for some, but it is likely that the same risks—and same outcomes—will be seen again before too long.

The GSK case is a good example of how changing political winds and market conditions can create an environment in which old risks, that were readily accepted as normal business practice, can be transformed into high-risk and potentially disastrous ones. Managers operating in the middle of the storm may be too involved to pause for thought, so corporate governance and strategic guidance, let alone legal compliance, need to be in place. And regular, independent due diligence is a good way for a far-off HQ to assess how risks are changing, and to adapt local operations accordingly.

Personal data disaster

Interestingly, the GSK case also shed (unwanted) light on the due diligence and investigations industry in China. Sources suggest that the impact has been wider than reported in the mainstream media, and that at least 200 China-based business intelligence operatives with some sort of link to the case may have been arrested, some on the back of evidence that they had possession of personal data, including confidential, official "hukou" reports. It is a reminder of the speed at which things can change—either because of high-level policy shifts or due to the initiative of a local official operating independently. Among those arrested were a British investigator in China, Peter Humphrey of ChinaWhys, and his business-partner wife. They reportedly got caught up in the GSK investigation having done work for the company in

China, and were arrested on July 10, 2013, and later jailed, for alleged misuse of personal data.[55] As noted in the Atlantic, there was an element or irony, in the arrests:

> Humphrey and his wife were accused not of corruption, but of violating a new law aimed at curbing corporate investigations. Police charged the couple with illegally purchasing personal information, including I.D. numbers, automobile and home ownership records, family member names and details of cross-border travel. Though the details are not public, GSK appeared to be employing ChinaWhys to ferret out the very corruption scandals for which the company is now being prosecuted.

As with the pharmaceutical example, the investigations business had been under increased scrutiny. In the Humphrey case there was a combination of increased awareness of personal privacy issues (including illegal trafficking of personal data) and growing sensitivity about the business dealings and wealth of high-profile political figures—especially after media reports connected to the families of some of China's top leadership. What had previously been common practice was no longer acceptable. Again the warning signs were there. In 2009 China updated its criminal code in order to control the use of personal information.[56] Then, in 2012 the China operations of a Dun & Bradstreet joint venture were closed down following a large number of arrests relating improper use of personal data.[57] According to The Compliance Blog[58]:

> On September 28, 2012, Dun & Bradstreet's local operating subsidiary Shanghai Roadway D&B Marketing Services Co., Ltd. ("Roadway") was charged by the Shanghai public prosecutor with "illegally obtaining private information from Chinese citizens." As reported by the Chinese press, the private information included the personal data of 150 million Chinese citizens, including their income, job titles, and addresses.

Also in 2012 there were moves to restrict access to the corporate data held by local offices of the State Administration of Industry & Commerce

(SAIC),[59] thereby potentially protecting Chinese companies from foreign short sellers such as Muddy Waters, as well as shareholders from having the value of their assets analyzed by prying eyes. Humphrey was of course aware of the changes, as he outlined in an article in *The Fraud Examiner*[60] in May 2013, just two months before his arrest:

> The promising environment that evolved for the fight against fraud and bribery in company operations in China has suffered a major setback due to a sudden government action to suppress certain data ... Critics describe this clampdown as an attempt to protect corrupt government officials from exposure. But as an anti-fraud worker in China serving purely corporate clients on corporate matters or in litigation support I find this a very dark day for due diligence and forensics work. I find this a step backwards that will make due diligence and catching fraudsters harder. We will have to be even more creative from now on.

Flexibility and creativity are essential to business survival in China, but sometimes the speed of change can take even the most experienced people by surprise—and the results can be devastating.

Supply chain pain

In December 2012, Yum Brands faced a consumer backlash after China Central Television (CCTV) reported that some of the company's suppliers in Shandong province had been injecting growth hormones and other additives into chicken sold through its KFC restaurants in China. A report on the issue in the *South China Morning Post*[61] covered the CCTV investigation. It included accusations that the chicken farms kept lights on all night to keep the birds feeding and growing faster, and that in addition to hormones, at least 18 types of antibiotic were administered to the chickens to keep them from getting sick.

As with many supply chains, it seems that KFC's was not simple. It was reported that individual farmers sold their chickens to a company called Liuhe Group in the city of Qingdao, and that Liuhe then supplied some

40 tonnes of chicken a month, direct to KFC (though KFC later ended the relationship). The farmers supplying Liuhe clearly knew something about what would be deemed acceptable, and had been fabricating documentation relating to their operations, and the conditions under which the chickens were being raised. KFC confirmed that it inspected its suppliers each year, applying strict assessment tests, and worked hard on damage limitation.

Sadly, as we know from the US-listed Chinese companies, documentation provided by people who want to defraud is often fraudulent! And despite the involvement of professional advisers or inspectors, it is not easy to see through muddied waters and to discover the truth, especially when the wrongdoing happens at the end of an extended supply chain.

The KFC case was far from being the first of its kind. Contamination of the supply chain for food has been a high-profile problem in China for some time, and it came to the fore with the widely reported scandal of melamine-tainted milk power, involving Sanlu and other producers around 2008.[62] It was also not the first issue of its kind for KFC in China. In 2005, KFC itself had been caught up in a food safety scandal involving the addition of Sudan 1 (or Sudan Red) industrial dyes into the supply chain of some of its products. At the time Danwei, a China blog,[63] reported on an apology from the company in the Beijing News:

> Despite having many times required our suppliers to guarantee that their products shouldn't contain Sudan I—and obtained their written confirmation—we are extremely sorry to admit that this ingredient has been discovered.

Danwei, knowing a thing or two about China, offered some free advice "maybe next time, aside from a written confirmation (hello, we're in China after all), Colonel Sanders should himself run tests on ingredients they feed to consumers." Others would be well advised to take the advice, or find themselves in the position of Aston Martin, which had to undertake a recall of 17,000 of its high-end cars in February 2014,[64] after it found that a supplier to a third-tier subcontractor had been producing counterfeit plastic parts. Once again, reliance on the honesty of others, and on the paperwork they provide, needs to be balanced with healthy skepticism, and the commercial likelihood that the supply chain is trying to protect its profits while faced with the simultaneous challenges of rising costs of production and downward price pressure from the customer.

Processes that protect businesses (and consumers) need to be put in place. Those processes should be designed and implemented by people with dirty hands and on-the-ground insights. They should involve people other than those managing the transaction, adapt to changing risks, and be used throughout a working relationship—not just at the start—so that there is protection from the time when profit pressures eventually start to squeeze quality standards.

Faking it: buy degrees

The Chinese education system is a tough and competitive one, with around seven million students graduating a year. For those that want to get the best jobs, there is an obvious temptation to short-circuit the system, to buy fake degrees, or to commit academic fraud. 2013 saw a slew of articles on academic fraud, including Wired: "China's academic scandal: call toll-free hotlines to get your name published."[65] A year earlier New Scientist also weighed in: "Fraud fighter: 'Faked research is endemic in China'."[66] In the same year nine people were put on trial in China for selling fake degrees from American universities.[67] The fake foreign degrees were provided at a premium, but fake Chinese degrees reportedly helped to fill the lower end of the market with more modest offerings. In other cases students have been scammed into buying what they believe to be authentic courses.

Senior executives are not immune from CV fraud,[68] and 2010 saw a heated debate over whether Jun Tang, a former head of Microsoft in China, had made a false claim (which he denied) about having a doctorate from the California Institute of Technology. Even technology guru Kai-fu Lee got embroiled in a debate over his experience[69] (though he seems to have done pretty well overall!). Foreigners too have been in the faking business, with faked teaching qualifications, and even fake foreign executives who get marched out to make proceedings look more international. One notable example[70] involved Canadian journalist and author Mitch Moxley, who, along with some other Westerners, was hired as a (fake) quality control expert. A fake quality controller is bad enough, but also in 2010 there were widespread reports[71] of 200 Chinese pilots having falsified their flying histories and CVs!

It is clear that competition to succeed combined with desire to share in the "Chinese dream" and to become gloriously rich provides fertile ground for faking. The fact that many executives hiring staff in China have relied on recommendations from their networks, have been too busy to check credentials, or have been confident in their own ability to judge applicants only makes matters worse. Increasingly, and in light of the stream of worrying examples, managers are becoming more aware, and are taking a more systematic approach to hiring graduates and senior employees. Many executive search firms include some form of background and qualification checks in their processes, while reputational and other checks can also be provided by specialist investigators.

Trademark trauma

Intellectual property rights (IPR) are usually right at the top of the list of worries for international companies operating in China (and for many Chinese companies in China too). Despite it being a common focus of risk analysis, even big firms sometimes suffer trauma.

The big trademark news of 2012 was the result of a three-year fight between US tech giant Apple and Proview Technology in Shenzhen.[72] The case was all about a little "i," and the rights to the iPad trademark in China that Apple had arranged to buy from Proview. As it turned out, it was actually a subsidiary of Proview in Shenzhen that owned the trademark, having registered it there in 2000—China being a first-to-file jurisdiction. The two companies entered into a lengthy legal battle which came to an end when Proview finally accepted payment (of a relatively modest) US$60 million from Apple. Stan Abraham of the China Hearsay blog[73] has pointed out that, despite all the noise around the case, it was not actually an IP one. But it was one with a due diligence lesson:

> this is NOT a case that imparts a lot of lessons for other foreign companies with IP issues … It was a breach of contract that happened to be about a trademark. This case did not involve the Trademark Law, Anti-unfair Competition Law or other IP rules or regulations, at least not directly … The only lesson here relates to the importance of due diligence, careful contract drafting, and post-agreement follow up.

It may not have technically been an IP case, but the IP registration issue is not a new one. China Law Blog's Dan Harris was almost shouting from the page when, in a 2007 post he wrote[74]:

> China is a first to register country and this means that whoever registers the trademark first gets it. Yes, there is an exception for famous trademarks, but unless you are Coca-Cola, it is lunacy to bank on a Chinese court holding your trademark is famous when just going ahead and registering it costs so little.

Understanding the rules, and being rigorous with due diligence at the outset can save a lot of pain later on. More comprehensive due diligence early on might have allowed Apple to dot the proverbial "i," saving a lot of face—and a lot of money.

Commercial crisis

Not all contracts are watertight (wherever they are enforced), and not all relationships are built to last. The case of an English businessman in the southern Chinese island-province of Hainan, famous for its beaches, was certainly no holiday. As reported in the *Financial Times*, a subsidiary of China Resources Group was[75]:

> accused of theft and illegal asset transfers in a previously unreported case involving British investors in the Chinese resort island of Hainan.

Keith Darby, a property developer, had set up a joint venture to develop a holiday resort on Hainan with China Resources in 2006. China Resources would have been a powerful local partner. Their Bloom World subsidiary's reported 3 per cent of the venture would not be expected to give it too much control but could help raise the profile of the development, and leverage their "guanxi" (connections) locally. However, things did not go according to plan and, after Darby missed a payment, Bloom World started arbitration proceedings. They were also accused of stealing the joint venture's official "chop" (seal), and of fraudulently transferring the company's assets at a fraction of the market value. Darby was left without access to the assets needed to pay his bills, and has had a challenging time competing with the once-valued guanxi of his erstwhile partners.

The case was ongoing at the time of writing, and is a reminder that reputational due diligence, while it may confirm the power of a prospective partner, should not ignore the flipside risk, and that keeping hold of the chops, which act as a key to the company's crown jewels, is critical. It is also a reminder of the risks involved with the joint-venture structure. Joint ventures in China have created historic headaches[76] for businesses as diverse as Danone (who fell out with Wahaha) and HSBC (whose investment in Bank of Communications suffered from post-deal regulatory restrictions). The list of joint-venture troubles started with one of the very first ones, *Beijing Jeep*,[77] and is likely to continue. Even a small shareholding can result in a big issue, and the structure itself needs careful due diligence treatment.

Risky Business in Brief: Bad News Is News

- *The risks are real, and there are plenty of examples to prove it*
- *There are often warning signs in the market, for those that watch*
- *Narrow, traditional due diligence can provide a false sense of security*
- *Due diligence is needed at the start, and throughout a relationship*
- *Uncertain legal enforcement increases the need for up-front risk management*

Chapter 3

Due Diligence in China

Due diligence approaches

Due diligence is a broad term, and a flexible tool. In China it is usually good to be flexible, and not to be bound by simple checklists and rigid rules. In the words of the famously flexible Bruce Lee[1]: "the stiffest tree is most easily cracked, while the bamboo or willow survives by bending with the wind."

The right timing, type, and amount of due diligence will vary depending on the type of driver (such as investment, M&A, sourcing or hiring), the project owner's approach to risk, and on the nature of the risk, including its size, value, and potential impact. Managers will have to decide not only what type of due diligence to conduct, but also when and how to do it. Should it include a focus on businesses, individuals, assets, operations, processes, policies, regulations, and/or other risks? Should it be proactive or reactive? Overt or covert? In-house or outsourced? The specifics will vary, but one thing is certain—due diligence is not optional! (See the Specialist Spotlight below).

In determining the risk factors that should be addressed, it is useful to consider which factors most often lead to failure, loss, and general pain in China businesses. Many of these things have as much to do with the principal as with the target, and many can be mitigated or avoided at the planning stage by being realistic, managing expectations, getting the right team in place, and setting down red lines that will not be crossed. Considerations include:

- Aims—if long-term aims are not aligned, it will not end well.
- Cultural fit—if it is not there, it will be hard to overcome obstacles.
- Communications—it is complex enough without misunderstandings.
- Information—if it is not there, or not accurate, it will not inform.
- Standards—unless clearly defined, assumptions and expectations may differ.
- Resources—are almost always tighter that predicted.
- Schedules—rushed deadlines reduce negotiation leverage and increase errors.
- Budgets—unexpected constraints can lead to cost and/or corner-cutting.
- Change—of people, policies, and market conditions mean moving goalposts.
- Optimism—is usually misplaced, and red flags should not be ignored!

Critically, the due diligence brief needs to fit the business aims and context. In some of the high-profile due diligence failures, the "right" answers may have been provided by the due diligence teams, but the wrong questions may have been asked of them. It is one thing to ask an accountant to review a set of accounts that has been provided by a prospective partner. It is quite another thing to ask if the accounts are consistent with the business operations, and whether there may be risks lurking around the corner. The former approach may work in some developed markets, where certain baseline assumptions can be made, but a more three-dimensional approach is needed in a market like China, where the numbers on the page may not add up in reality.

Some businesses recognize the need for due diligence but try to address it too narrowly as they don't want to kill the deal, or as they want to save on fees. However it is important to look at a variety of risks, from internal operational issues to the potentially catastrophic external ones (think SARS[2]), and to ensure that the business can adapt. For some supply chains it is a process that could take years to plan and develop, and for some companies it has been happening slowly but surely since at least 2008, according to Katherine Peavy who also notes that it is important to have an exit strategy, in case the risks look like they could start to outweigh the rewards. She also points out that the cost of due diligence is easy to quantify and so can seem expensive in relation to the unquantifiable cost of the potential risk. Taking a long view, and with reference to reported cases of actual losses, companies would be well advised to put a figure on the risk cost, before trying to save money on preventative measures.

Kent Kedl believes too many people are too binary in their approach to due diligence in China, seeing only win and lose scenarios. In his experience less than five per cent of deals suffer death by due diligence, while those that pass the tests are able to move on with the benefit of business intelligence and confidence. The "third way" is the more usual outcome, with deals being restructured on the basis of due diligence findings in around 60 per cent of cases. A practical and positive approach to the brief, combined with flexibility in response to the results, is generally the best approach.

Proactive or reactive

Due diligence can, and should be, proactive. A proactive approach based on sound procedures can help to identify and address risks before they become a problem. The work can be budgeted, resourced, and scheduled for in good time, avoiding a last-minute squeeze and a rushed job. It can be deployed during pre-acquisition processes, pre-contract negotiations, or before new staff are signed. It can also be, and often is, reactive. This happens when responding to changes in the business or regulatory environment, assessing newly identified risks, when issues are brought to light by whistleblowers (as is increasingly the case), when scandals erupt in the media (or CCTV highlights failures of consumer protection at another major multinational), following failed audits, accidents, disastrous investments, or when people or things go missing.

Kedl refers to the "oh shit" moment as being a common trigger for managers to reactively call in some due diligence support. But it is often too late. Due diligence should also be applied from the strategy development stage in China, but very few give it sufficient, proactive consideration early on, when some external red-flag analysis could have a significant impact, and save a lot of problems, later. In general it is best to plan to be proactive but be ready to be reactive. China is a challenging place to do business, and even the best-laid plans sometimes need urgent, real-time rethinking.

SPECIALIST SPOTLIGHT: CHINA DUE DILIGENCE—NOT OPTIONAL

Dan Harris of Harris Moure/China Law Blog[3]

A US company goes to China and meets with a company there for manufacturing product. The two parties sign an agreement and US company sends over a large sum of money to build the tooling.

The Chinese company then says another large sum is needed to be ready to go as soon as the tooling is complete. Months pass. Nothing. More months pass. Nothing. It has now been a year and still nothing.

The US Company contacts my firm and wants to know about pursuing litigation against this Chinese manufacturer to recover the money paid. We determine that the US company has a very strong case, but suggest we first investigate the Chinese company to determine whether it has sufficient assets to pursue.

We conduct a fast and cheap investigation and get a comprehensive report on the Chinese company. From this report we learn the following: The company is not a manufacturer. It is a trader, with a tiny, rented office. It does not even have an export license. In other words, it gets its products from manufacturers and then has to bring on another company to ship them. It is just a middle-person. Its only asset is a small amount of inventory, which it may or may not own.

The US company then decides to order a comprehensive report on ALL of the Chinese companies with which it presently conducts business.

Perhaps you should too. China due diligence. Not optional.

Don't ignore warning signs[4]

Overt or covert

Depending on the risk owner's aims, the status of negotiations, and the relationship with a counterparty, the issue of due diligence may be considered a risk factor in itself. There is often a fear that the due diligence target might be offended by the idea, with loss of face, especially if a lot of time and effort (and food and drink) has already gone into establishing a friendly professional relationship.

A covert due diligence approach might be preferable in the early stages of project development, when working out a short list of targets, where plans are still confidential, or when initial contact has been made, but before serious commitments are in place. Covert due diligence can also be used later on in the process, for specific issues that present themselves as red flags. "Covert" does not necessarily imply a Bond-style thriller, or sneaky subterfuge. It just means that legitimate research and fact checking is done without the knowledge of the target. As a result, although the available information may be limited, the advantage is that as the target is not involved, the focus and process of information collection can be controlled by the principal, and the information received will include objective research and analysis of the situation on the ground, independent third-party opinions, and verified official information (such as that which can be obtained from the Administration of Industry and Commerce).

Overt, or open, due diligence is an equally important tool, especially where full disclosure of confidential company information is required, such as "hard" details of accounts, assets, liabilities, products, customers, and business plans. The core parts of the traditional legal and financial due diligence processes are, by necessity, open, as they require the target to provide access to commercially sensitive information. A covert attempt to obtain such details would involve not only moral hazard, but also legal risk of breaking laws around commercial secrets (or, in the case of State Owned Enterprises, even state secrets). The case of "The Rio Tinto Four," in which four employees were imprisoned in China in 2010, is an example that got much attention at the time, and which pointed to tighter regulation of foreign firms' activities, especially in important areas of the economy. As *The New York Times* reported[5]:

> "The Rio Tinto case is sending a signal to the world, that China's model of managing its financial activities has changed," said Liu Junhai, a professor of law at Renmin University in Beijing. "In the past, we overemphasized the country's development, but didn't pay enough attention to regulation."

Investigate or review

Both overt and covert due diligence should involve elements of investigative work. At the most basic level investigations involve simple desk research, but they can also involve detailed research that seeks to verify known or assumed facts or risks through activities such as (legitimate) data acquisition, interviews with a range of people with direct or indirect knowledge about the target, as well as legal, asset, product or service reviews, site visits, and reputation checks. The process also requires analysis and cross-referencing of findings that can help to join the data dots, and make sense of what might initially be a very faint outline of a picture.

Legal and financial due diligence are generally accepted requirements for business, and are served by armies of lawyers and accounts in every corner of China, and the world. They are essential, but can also be expensive, process- and document-driven, relying to a great extent on review of information provided by the target of the due diligence (think back to all those New York-listed Chinese companies). Given the generally invasive nature, and the level of investment required, of the formal processes, it makes sense to phase the due diligence process, starting with the more informal research, building into issues requiring investigation and then, only when the target is confirmed to pass muster, call in the big guns. The phased approach can save a lot of time, money, and wasted effort—Kroll in China have estimated that around 10 per cent of transactions involving legal and financial due diligence are terminated due to the findings of investigative due diligence.[6]

David Cogman, a Partner in McKinsey's office in Shanghai[7] underlines the importance of tailoring risk management processes to the Chinese environment, noting that while "everyone transacting in China needs to go through the traditional, formal due diligence process, it may not actually help. Investigative due diligence needs to be added in order to validate the findings." He notes that problems with China-specific things, such as certain permits, may be red lines in a traditional Western due diligence sense but require some flexibility in the less legalistic Chinese context, as many issues can be resolved if approached in the right way. He stresses that "due diligence in China is not a hoop-jumping process. It is neither sufficient nor helpful tick the boxes and say 'yes we've done it, here is the report'." People need to be eyeballed, assets confirmed, and operations looked at by experienced practitioners who can read the context and judge the risk.

Legitimate investigations will normally start with a public domain sweep, using key words, aliases, and other relevant terms. "It all comes down to chronology and connections," according to Rupert Utley,[8] who was originally in the Royal Hong Kong Police, before working as a partner with Deloitte & Touche and other professional service firms on complex investigations. Along with the specialist divisions of the big accounting firms, Utley uses sophisticated systems to manage and interrogate large volumes of data, and then focuses on getting out to speak to key people, and look at things, on the ground. He also cautions that data security needs to be addressed as even some innocuous business intelligence could look like "state secrets" if it relates to a state-owned enterprise. This is one reason why some companies think carefully about where and how data is collected and stored—especially since the Rio Tinto case. Hai Yang, founder of Beijing Steele Business Investigation Centre,[9] is a veteran of the China investigations business, and of the Beijing Public Security Bureau. He has also warned that there is a need to be careful with investigation processes, and with the handling of information gathered:

> Information is diversified. Confidential information is just one kind. It can be classified into four types according to different levels: national confidential information, personal private information, business secret information and other protected information. Each country has corresponding laws and regulations to protect such kinds of information. Except for the above four types, other information is all public. Therefore, some people may ask whether they can abuse the information if it is obtained legally. The answer is … maybe. If the information we get by legal means has a very negative impact on the people involved, we are much more likely to bear the responsibility for infringing upon their civil rights.

> The information we use must be public and legal. Confidential information obtained from any means cannot be legally used in any situation without the authorization by the information owner.

In one case Utley was working on behalf of an accounting firm in a major dispute relating to electronics products that were produced around Dongguan in Guangdong province. The only way to progress the investigation was to (literally) go through all sorts of official doors and to approach people with open questions. Many are happy to address legitimate questions, at least to some extent, and one senior customs official, while he did not divulge any confidential information, was able to suggest where the relevant records could (legally) be accessed, what records could only be seen by a registered lawyer, and what would be confidential or a state secret and therefore arrestable territory. Some information may be "private" and off-limits, while some is "public" but hidden in plain sight. A guide is needed in order to find the invisible door in the proverbial brick wall.

It would be a trusting person who blindly accepts that "the truth, the whole truth, and nothing but the truth" (as the English courts put it) will always be disclosed on the basis of a polite request to a potential business partner or acquisition target who is commercially motivated to get the deal done. At worst, falsified documents and records may be produced, but even an attempt to put their best foot forward, or to hide (or just ignore) something that is not considered important (by them), or which could result in loss of face (something that contradicts an early assertion, a bit of dark history, or other issue) could lead to major headaches later.

In-house or out-source

Once the need for due diligence has been accepted (it is always needed to some degree), it needs to be delivered, and managers will have to balance their resource, budget, or confidentiality constraints with their risk appetite. There are a number of checklists and tools that can be used to help scope out the requirements, but a key consideration will be whether to conduct the work internally or externally, or using both internal and external resources. Either way, a successful result will depend on the skills and experience of the people involved.

There are large numbers of local and foreign, large and small service providers operating in China, including the big international legal, accounting, risk firms, a range of smaller, but well-established firms set up by long-term "China hands," some of them formerly with the big blue-chip companies, that can provide specialist services without the high overheads bigger firms have to cover in their fees. There are also a variety of Chinese firms, ranging from law and accounting firms that compete with the multinationals, to those that have a specialist focus and/or local footprint. And the footprint can be a critical issue, given the diversity of China's business landscape, the geographic location of sector clusters, varying dialects, and guanxi networks.

Many of the services required to conduct due diligence can be procured at a modest financial cost, and with a huge saving in terms of management time and opportunity cost. If the work is to be done internally, it is useful to ensure that the right skills are available, that more than one person is involved, and that enough time and budget is made available. It is also wise to consider the cost (and corporate and personal) implications of things going wrong. Before making a decision on how to handle a case, it is useful to make a basic cost comparison, including the cost of internal resource time, travel and information expenses, and the cost of contracting out some or all of the services. The life of a manager in China can be busy and challenging enough, without trying to control every detail of a complicated due diligence project. For example it would almost never make sense to try and obtain Administration of Industry and Commerce (AIC) records using internal resources, as access is limited to qualified people such as locally registered lawyers, the location may be inconvenient, and the time required would be hard to measure. On the other hand, the information may be held on a credit company's database, or be available within a few days, at minimal cost using an external service provider.

If some or all of the work is outsourced, it can often be done by a single firm with a range of internal resources. However, it may be necessary, or beneficial (for confidentiality, specialist skills availability, diverse target locations, or other reasons) to use a number of contractors to cover issues such as credit checks, litigation checks, site visits, third-party interviews, or other activities. In such cases, a resource and project plan is needed to ensure efficient scheduling and co-ordination of the work. However the information is obtained, it is important that the recipient has the knowledge to scope out the right brief and to draw sensible conclusions from the results. And there is often value in having a pair of fresh, objective eyes evaluate risks that might be missed by someone who already has a lot invested in a successful businesses outcome.

Table 3.1 outlines an example of the flow of due diligence activities might be applied in practice when seeking to work with a new supplier or partner. The activities can be divided into preliminary covert research and background checks, and overt verification work that requires access to the targets facilities, management, and other information.

Table 3.1 Example of due diligence process

Process	Type	Activity	Resource	Cost	Week
Screening	Covert	Online checks	Internal	Low	1
	Covert	Credit checks	External	Low	2
Evaluation	Covert	Litigation checks	External	Low	3
	Covert	Media checks	External	Low	3
	Covert	Site visits	External	Low	3
	Covert	Pretext calls	Internal/ External	Low	3
	Covert	Reputation checks	Internal/ External	Medium	3
Engagement	Overt	Reference checks	Internal/ External	Low	4
	Overt	Management/ Staff meetings	Internal	Low	4
	Overt	Financial checks	Internal/ External	Medium	4+
	Overt	Operations checks	Internal/ External	Low	4+
	Overt	Inspections/ testing	Internal/ External	Low	4+
Operation	Overt	Inspections/ testing	Internal/ External	Low	Quarterly +
	Overt	Management meetings	Internal	Low	Quarterly +
	Overt	Site visits	Internal	Low	Annually +
	Covert	Pretext calls	Internal/ External	Low	Annually +
	Covert	Credit checks	External	Low	Annually +
	Covert	Compliance checks	Internal/ External	Low	Annually +

The timing of due diligence activities can vary depending on the aims of the project, visibility and size of the target, the budget and resources available, and any time constraints. Where budgets and internal resources are limited, it makes sense to phase the work, and limit inputs at each stage. So online research could be done in-house in order to filter down to a short list of targets, before credit checks are outsourced in order to qualify the priority target list. Once a smaller pool of targets is confirmed, litigation and media checks can be commissioned, and other activities such as site visits, reputation checks, and pretext calls can be undertaken. In cases where time is more constrained than budget, it is usually possible to turn around the screening and evaluation processes within seven to ten days, using the services of an external contractor.

Risky Business in Brief: Due Diligence Approaches

- *Due diligence processes need to be adapted to suit Chinese conditions*
- *Plan around time and resource constraints—and for the unexpected*
- *Set appropriate scope and focus, and look beyond box ticking and documents*
- *Phase the work, and use external specialists where necessary*
- *Remain objective and don't ignore red flags*

Due diligence types

There are a number of due diligence types that can be classified by functional focus. They range from high-level to specific, and objective to subjective, subject-driven to principal-driven, and from box-ticking to lid-lifting. They commonly include the following, sometimes overlapping, types:

- Political and regulatory
- Commercial
- Operational
- Legal
- Financial
- Compliance
- Environmental, health, safety and social
- Reputational
- Personal

Whether, and to what extent these options are applied in a given case, will depend on the purpose—whether for sourcing, manufacturing, M&A, employment, or other reason—the scale, and risk context.

Political and regulatory

China is a political beast, with the Party at its heart, and the importance of political and regulatory due diligence cannot be overstated. In the context of managing political risk Kerry Brown, Professor of Chinese Politics and Director of the China Studies Centre at the University of Sydney, remarks on the role of the Party and suggests that it is the Chinese government's own risk management tool, focused on maintaining growth and stability while also trying to juggle a regular stream of man-made and natural crises. He notes that big companies need to have a strategy for dealing with the Party—avoidance is impossible—not only for external, high-level engagement, but also internally and locally.

Stability is a traditional political aim in China, and the Chinese government has overseen a long period of stable growth. While more stability may be expected, risks always remain. McKinsey's Asia Chairman, Gordon Orr, advises[10] that, while some risks may not be probable: "It's not good enough to be prepared for volatility; we must anticipate different kinds of volatility." Some of the different kinds of volatility-inducing risks that might be considered as part of the due diligence process include issues as diverse as the anti-corruption campaign, economic restructuring, high levels of debt, a property bubble, wealth inequality, health, the environment, natural disasters, separatist terrorism, and regional tensions. The Eurasia Group puts China risk at number three in its Top Risks for 2014, a list which focuses on "the most challenging political and geopolitical stress points for global investors and market participants"[11]:

> The new China: The country's leaders have initiated the most far-reaching reforms in two decades. But the Communist Party will face formidable political tests given the increasingly hard-to-control information environment and backlash from those who stand to lose from economic rebalancing. Missteps could undermine reform and the leadership itself.

Bilateral risk also comes into the equation for businesses, as a political spat with Beijing can result in foreign leaders being given a cold shoulder, as has been experienced in the recent past by a number of countries, including the UK and Norway. While this sort of treatment may delay the mega missions of CEOs and ministers that regularly arrive in Beijing, it does not always have a catastrophic impact for business. The UK had a long period without any ministerial visits following David Cameron's meeting with the Dalai Lama in May 2012, but the UK saw impressive trade growth and a record amount of Chinese inbound investment during the same period. As the China Daily reported in December 2013[12]:

> From January to October, China–UK bilateral trade continued to grow and Registered an increase of 7.5 percent with a total volume of $56.1 billion … In the past year and a half, Chinese investments exceeded the total of the previous three decades.

That said, there can be mysterious coincidences in the timing of Presidential visits and the resolution of commercial disputes. During

President Xi Jinping's visit to Europe in March 2014 Airbus signed a 10-year deal for aircraft assembly in China while also unblocking US$6 billion worth of orders that had been in limbo since the EU imposed charges on aircraft emissions.[13] China also agreed to end an anti-dumping and anti-subsidy investigation into exports of European wine.[14]

To some extent the high-level political impact for foreign business can be assessed by referencing the government's stated plans, as China is usually quite clear about its policy and economic objectives. APCO's[15] December 2010 analysis of the 12th five-year plan (FYP), running from 2011 to 2015 noted[16]:

> The 12th FYP's guiding principles will promote the government's focus on "inclusive growth," which means ensuring the benefits of economic growth are spread to a greater proportion of Chinese citizens. The plan's key themes are rebalancing the economy, ameliorating social inequality and protecting the environment.

The detail behind the themes previewed what has since been seen - slower growth rates, a move away from reliance on investment and exports and towards consumption, increased minimum wages, expansion of health insurance, and improved energy efficiency. The report highlighted the plan's benefits for the healthcare, energy and technology sectors, but also questioned how far foreign firms would be able to benefit given the "indigenous innovation" policy. Increased costs from wages, price reforms, taxes, and environmental costs were also flagged. Since 2010, the planning has progressed, and refined messages on issues such as economic and market reforms, state-owned enterprises, the rule of law, anti-corruption, urbanization, and the environment were delivered at the November 2013 Third Plenum,[17] and the March 2014 National People's Congress (NPC).[18] As reported by Xinhuanet after the Third Plenum[19]:

> A significant theory of the session was to acknowledge the market's decisive role in allocating resources ...However, Xi noted that to let the market decide does not mean to let it decide all.

At a macro and at a sector level it is important for businesses to listen and react to the messages that are sent out from Beijing.

W. John Hoffmann, co-founder of Exceptional Resources Group (XRG)[20] in Hong Kong, is a former merchant banker and experienced China specialist. Hoffmann's XRG focuses on major cross-border deals involving Chinese interests, especially "impossible and difficult" ones that are complex or involve highly regulated industries. In Hoffmann's experience, novel transactions in China—typically ones where there is a vacuum in terms of policy and precedent—require "top-down" acceptance from China's Communist Party leaders.

"As China is a rule-of-man, not a rule-of-law, civilization-state, if businesses don't get to grips with the politics and personalities, they are making a fundamental error." To illustrate the point, Hoffmann points out that the ubiquitous China Daily government chart (designed by XRG together with Edelman and China Daily in 1995, and revised and published periodically ever since) does not represent the political and policy-making power structure within China; rather, according to Hoffmann, the key leaders in the government organization chart need to be viewed in the context of their Party positions and performance— "their family backgrounds, political mentors and their factional affiliations help define their personal political power and likely impact on policies and projects, not only in Beijing but also at district, city and provincial levels." XRG started tracking the "5th Generation" of rising Party and government leaders in 2006, at the prompting of a multinational client that was well established in China, and launched a major research project[21] to better understand the people in the Party power structures. Since Party politics has such an enormous impact on business in China, Hoffmann reasons that businesses need to pay serious attention to the 205 full members of the Communist Party's 18th Central Committee:

> If a multinational company does not know which ones are relevant to them, and how, and if they are not tracking the rising stars of the next generation, then they are just left guessing ... you need to start with an over-the-horizon analysis of the political power structure, and the individuals within it.

Some multinationals, including GSK, have found themselves sailing into a perfect storm of commercial, legal, and political risks. It is hard to predict the future, but Kerry Brown reinforces the need to know the background of the people in power, noting that Xi Jinping has had an anti-corruption agenda for 20 years and that his continuing focus on it now that he is in power should not have been a surprise. It should also not be a surprise that strategic sectors such as oil and gas and pharmaceuticals are being targeted, as the leadership believes they have lost vast sums of money to enrich a few at the expense of the nation, and that they need to deliver more efficiency and value in the future. The GSK case shows that the risks are real, and are important for businesses to address. It involved an industry that is considered sensitive due to its impact on the (ageing and health-challenged) population, and because there are big foreign companies with dominant positions. The government's policies to reform the sector by expanding healthcare coverage and lowering costs increased the political risks but did not change the industry's entrenched local operating practices, which have long been considered risky. The anti-corruption campaign added legal risks to the mix. There was a Beijing-driven policy push on a sector level, a national campaign to tackle bribery and corruption, and a local legal issue that was addressed by a zealous Public Security Bureau. So, whatever the details of the specific case, risk assessment needs to include long-term, macro considerations, policy change, and the legal environment. Too narrow a focus on a business target will miss the dangers posed by the wider context.

China has been very strategic in its development plan, and has specific categories for inward investors that are outlined in its Catalogue for the Guidance of Foreign Investment Industries,[22] and which range from "encouraged" to "prohibited." Initially attracting foreign investment in manufacturing with incentives and tax breaks, China gradually opened up the domestic market, before focusing more on R&D, "indigenous innovation" and certain strategic industries, along with overseas direct investment and technology acquisition. Foreign companies have been welcome to play their part in the economic development plan, and to profit from it. But as the need for foreign investment and know-how has decreased, so has the attitude to foreign firms changed. One example of a foreign firm that has had to adapt to a changing China is Wal-Mart, who set up in south China's Guangdong, as far away from Beijing's political power as possible. While such an approach may have worked in the US, in China it failed to account for Beijing's personalities and political risks. The situation got serious in 2004 when they became involved in a politically charged spat over the role of unions in their (and other foreign) business, something a million dollar donation could not do much to cure. According to *China Daily*[23]:

> The US retail giant Wal-Mart invested one million US dollars to establish China's first retail research centre at Beijing's prestigious Tsinghua University.

> The move came just days after China's trade union authority threatened to blacklist Wal-Mart for refusing to establish union branches ... officials with the All-China Federation of Trade Unions (ACFTU) said they will blacklist and possibly sue foreign companies that are reluctant to set up trade unions in their China facilities. Wal-Mart, Dell, Kodak, Samsung and some KFC and McDonald's restaurants were among the companies ACFTU mentioned.

The decreasing political attractiveness, and increased competitive risk, associated with foreign investment continued to grow, and by 2006 Li Deshui, then head of the National Bureau of Statistics, said[24]:

> If we allow the free development of malicious acquisitions by multinational companies, the autonomous brands and innovative ability of China's national industry will gradually disappear.

As noted at the time[25]:

> [T]his sort of language is always intended to deliver a serious message ... it may also be a sign of the times that foreign and domestic tax rates in China are set to be harmonized, and that foreign firms have been accused of "immense" tax evasion by a member of the Chinese People's Political Consultative Conference (CPPCC) ... It might therefore also be wise to keep an eye on the development

of China's Anti-Monopoly Law, which is set to be published this year. And, for good measure, why not spare some time for public relations and corporate social responsibility programmes. After all, foreign businesses benefit themselves, and local interests, when they contribute to the communities and countries in which they operate.

Fast forward to 2014, the balance of power has moved further to the Chinese side, which holds an enormous market, and which wants to develop its own strong companies and brands so that it can both serve the people and retain some profit. This is especially true as China extends its influence beyond its borders, for example with the Anti-Monopoly Law (AML). China has already shown its appetite for reviewing the impact of global M&A deals in China. According to Reuters, China's Ministry of Commerce (MOFCOM) had reviewed 750 AML cases between the AML's introduction in 2008 and February 2014. Freshfields noted in August 2013 that[26]:

> MOFCOM is regularly intervening in high-profile global transactions. This trend is expected to continue. The lack of certainty as well as transparency of the MOFCOM review process may cause practical challenges to companies contemplating international transactions ... As MOFCOM is also increasingly confident in taking a different approach from that taken by other major competition authorities and as non-competition factors appear to play a role in the review process, companies should not assume that just because other agencies have unconditionally cleared their transaction or because, from a purely competition analysis perspective, there do not appear to be any substantive issues, that their cases will not prove to be problematic in China.

The first global transaction that felt the impact of a MOFCOM review was the 2008 Anheuser-Busch—InBev merger, which was subject to conditions imposed by China,[27] including a ban on Anheuser-Busch and InBev increasing their stakes in Tsingdao Brewery and Zhujiang Brewery, respectively, as well as a ban on additional investments in two of the leading Chinese beer brands. Other recent review cases with conditions imposed have included:

- Glencore/Xtrata, 2012
- Google/Motorola, 2012
- Seagate/Samsung, 2012
- Walmart/Niuhai, 2012
- Marubeni/Gavilon, 2013

As of early 2014, China had only rejected one deal outright—the proposed 2009 acquisition of Chinese drinks company Huiyuan by Coca-Cola, on the basis that Coca-Cola could have leveraged its dominant market position in the carbonated drinks market into the juice market in which Huiyuan is a leader.

Any sensible foreign company engaged in a deal that might come under AML scrutiny should seek to understand and align with policy, lobby and get feedback from relevant officials, avoid obvious conflicts or previously reported problems, proactively engage on information delivery and negotiation, and pay attention to the likely impact of the MOFCOM review timing. In the 2013 AMD/Grain Corp case, the proposed deal included a structure that specifically accounted for anticipated AML-driven delays.

In addition to major international merger review, China has become increasingly active in anti-trust cases at home. *Want China Times* reported in March 2014 that[28]:

> [G]overnment agencies monitoring market prices investigated 34,400 cases that involved manipulating prices, with economic sanctions reaching 3.1 billion yuan (US$511 million). Of the amount, 632 million yuan (US$103.1 million) was refunded to consumers, while combined illegal gains of 907 million yuan (US$148 million) were seized.

In early 2014, US companies Qualcomm and InterDigital were targeted, while, in August 2013, baby milk power makers, including Mead

Johnson, Danone, and Fonterra, were fined US$110 million for price and anti-competitive violations.[29] Coming after serious milk powder scandals disrupted the domestic industry, perhaps the increased scrutiny of leading foreign firms should not have come as a surprise.

Transfer pricing has also attracted more attention, with PwC noting[30] that the Chinese tax authority the State Administration of Taxation (SAT) has been "enforcing stringent strong local-flavoured transfer pricing regulations/rules." Bloomberg's Transfer Pricing Watch[31] adds that regulation and enforcement in China is expected to increase over the next few years, and that for 2014 the SAT has stated it will focus on:

- *Guo Shui Fa [2009] No.2 (Circular 2):* revision of China's core transfer pricing regulations
- *General anti-avoidance:* clarification and continued work on detailed guidelines on this topic
- *Services transactions:* issuance of guidelines on intercompany services transactions
- *Equity transfer:* clarifications on requirements and processes on intercompany equity transfers, such as its preference for the income approach for valuations.

In sensitive sectors the risk impact of policy and regulation can be obvious, and innovative approaches do not always work out. Mark Kitto, and his "That's" group of magazines is a case in point[32]—it started with him putting together an unprecedented China publishing deal, but ended with his unceremonious ouster by a powerful local partner. In other sectors the risks can be harder to foresee, and can be driven by social issues as much as by multinational non-compliance. An example is the sudden ban on the use of mobile apps for finding taxis in Beijing and Shanghai—they were deemed unfair and allowed official price controls to be avoided.[33] In an industry that has attracted millions of investment dollars, the impact will be felt by (very frustrated) consumers as well as investors ... who would be wise to consider how far their innovative technologies may prove an irritation to local regulators. On a larger scale, and with significant strategic impact for business, China has over the past few years been restricting exports of rare earths (China, as with many things, is the largest producer), while also consolidating the local industry and expanding processing capacity. The stated purpose of the restrictions was to protect the environment, but there are suggestions of wider commercial issues at play, and that China has also used the policy as a response to bilateral spats (such as with Japan in 2010). In March 2014 the *Financial Times* reported on the decision by a World Trade Organization (WTO) panel[34]:

> that export taxes and other restrictions China began to impose on so-called rare earths in 2009 were in violation of WTO rules.

Kent Kedl stresses the fact that risk management needs to go beyond legal issues in China, and that political and regulatory risks which can have industry-wide implications need to be addressed proactively. Too many companies fail to invest in real government relationship-building. When a policy or regulatory-driven crisis hits there is often a panic as people realize that their government relationships are too reactive, narrow, and shallow to facilitate any real dialogue or understanding. Kedl recommends scenario planning, so that swift and appropriate action can be taken should the worst occur. Political and regulatory due diligence needs to be regularly updated on a country and industry level, as well as on an individual level, as the macro environment and the regulations are constantly changing, and as the important political connection of today may be the corrupt former official of tomorrow.

A stark reminder of this need was provided by the case of Bo Xilai, who was removed as Party Secretary of Chongqing in March 2012, amidst a scandal that involved, among other things, the death of a British businessman. The Bo issue raised some interesting and difficult questions for China watchers. Hoffmann's analysis led to his early 2012 prediction that the new government of Xi Jinping would embark on a new anti-corruption campaign, pinioned around the "Rule of Law."[35] In Hoffmann's view, foreign businesses are politically expendable targets for Chinese anti-corruption, anti-monopoly, and other legal actions and can be used as the proverbial chicken in the Chinese tradition of "killing the chicken to scare the monkey." Under the circumstances, Hoffmann recommends constant political and regulatory vigilance.

Foreign companies are a useful target for sending the message that corruption and market abuse will not be tolerated, especially in strategic or sensitive sectors where foreign firms dominate. Further down the line local interests will feel the stick too, but most likely only once they have grown a bit stronger, and can take the beating without too much damage being done. Businesses that that turn a blind eye to changes in policy focus and regulatory detail risk walking into a minefield of risks.

Risky Business in Brief: Political and Regulatory Due Diligence

- *Government, and the Party and policy are part of business reality*
- *Align strategy with long-term government plans*
- *Political personalities, as well as policies, require analysis*
- *Relationships with government should not rely on one person*
- *Foreign firms will be held to a higher standard than local ones*

Commercial

Commercial due diligence is a natural starting point for risk management in China, once the political and regulatory environment is confirmed to be friendly, as it allows for an objective view of the market context and tests the most basic levels of health and attraction. Suwei Jiang, a Partner in the China Business Group at PwC in the UK,[36] underlines the importance of standing back from a deal, and using commercial due diligence at the start of the process to ensure that a target's business model and operational claims makes sense. Where (as has been the case) a company reports 20 to 30 per cent profit growth a year, it is worth looking around the market, and asking whether the claims are realistic.

If properly planned, commercial due diligence can be designed into the research that forms part of the partner/supplier/acquisition target selection process. Stefan Kracht, Managing Director of Fiducia Management Consultants,[37] which has operated for over 30 years in China, suggests that before getting into any details it is best to check that the big picture makes sense in terms of:

- Wider market conditions, including economic and political trends and risks.
- Growth and trends in the sector, including potential regulatory impact.
- Competitive positioning and potential of the target within the sector.

Unless a target can get over the commercial market test bar, it is unlikely to be useful as a long-term acquisition or partner, whatever other type of due diligence it is able to pass. A legally perfect partner will provide little benefit if it is dying a slow, painful death-by-market. And while it may not seem to be suffering now, it is necessary to judge whether it will be able to bear the potential post-deal burdens of new (guanxi-less) relationships, new (international) standards, new (FCPA/Bribery Act) compliance requirements, higher (staffing) costs, and other (usually costly) issues. The very real post-deal problems mean that thought is also required for how the paper deal will work in practice, and how it will be managed to ensure that existing competitive advantages are not lost in transition.

Bearing in mind the importance of selecting the right target, and testing its foundations, Kracht suggests it is best to use the lens of commercial due diligence to look at it in a broad, rather than narrow, context. This means including suppliers, customers, and stakeholders in

the scope of the work. It also requires the principal to be
clear about the red lines it will not cross, and to set some
walk-away criteria from the start. There can always be
some flexibility (this is China, after all), but there
is a danger that compromise can blur important
red lines once "deal fatigue" sets in, and when the end
is tantalizingly near. It is also best to maintain options throughout the
process. If there is only one serious candidate to test, the principal risks
losing the ability to assess any identified risks objectivity, as they would
risk killing the only deal in the game. The target, by comparison, would
see its hand getting stronger the further in they get, either offsetting
the negative impact of risk (on which the principal is reluctant to act),
or simply reinforcing their dominant position. As Andrew Hupert of
China Solved puts it[38]:

> Chinese negotiators aren't susceptible to logic or pressure—since
> most of the time they start off believing (correctly or not) that their
> position is stronger than yours. When you are dealing with a Chinese
> counterparty, the only options you have are to stay at the table or
> walk away. If you are going to convince them that your threats of
> withdrawal are credible, then you have to have a realistic, plausible
> option at your disposal. The only way to be convincing—and per-
> suasive—is to have a Plan B ready before you sit down.

The natural selection process, from industry mapping (which may
include 200 to 300 companies for a larger transaction) to long list
review (30 to 50 companies) and short list qualification (four to six),
provides valuable options. It is also a process that forces objectivity into
what may already be a cosy relationship between a foreign company
and a Chinese supplier seeking to move from being "just friends" to
being bound by marriage. Even if the principal remains loyal to the old
friend, at least there will be some independent benchmarks to highlight
areas of strength and weakness. And the intended target will not be
able to sit pretty, in the knowledge that there are no other suitors to
contend with.

A Change of direction may be needed[39]

But rather than using the due diligence discovery process as stick with which to beat a partner into submission, it can be used more strategically and effectively as a way to build communication, deepen understanding, and ensure that a stable relationship can result. Commercial due diligence also benefits from being less formal and invasive than legal or financial due diligence, so can take a softer and more business-oriented approach. Fiducia finds that the process itself can bridge the gaps between parties, and that this is best done with small building blocks. The Western approach to due diligence is generally more detailed, paper-based and formal. These ingredients are not ideal for making a deal work in China. Instead, more face time is needed for relationship-building, as well as more extensive triangulation of information sources (including staff, suppliers, and customers) in order to get the full picture.

Instead of focusing on the end-game, and the big issues, it helps to work through a schedule of more manageable milestones that can be used to generate positive interactions and outcomes. It also allows for regular, and sometimes extended, site visits so that operations are not just seen in their pristine, public moments, but as the day-to-day operations and issues are dealt with. Trust can be built, and reliability demonstrated on both side.

Some prospective Chinese partners will be very open in relation to the sharing of information, and often don't even require a confidentiality agreement to be in place during initial discussions. Some try to reveal too much in a desire to impress, but it is an intellectual property red flag if they start to share details of confidential plans or designs for their customers. Information generally may be less secure than foreign visitors imagine, especially given the range of guanxi networks that spread through Chinese industries via companies, universities, and research institutes. In one case Kracht found that two seemingly unrelated company owners in north and south China had been speaking to each other about a principal's acquisition plans. The second seem very well prepared!

Once into detailed analysis, third-party verification work can be done using online and AIC resources, as well as by using visits to the local Labour office and Public Security Bureau. In addition to checking relevant documents, it is worth listening carefully to the responses given by officials, as they may provide subtle indications if and where further attention should be focused. A review of operations can confirm the validity of ISO and test certifications (issuers can also be contacted), while quality control processes and work-flow charts can provide insight into the practical workings of a business. For commonly questioned issues such as the validity of financial reports, Kracht recommends focusing on the sales figures (and the related chain of internal documentation) and identifying areas where they do not match the officially recorded figures. In the same way, looking at staff records and contracts can help ensure that everything is in order.

Should an acquisition look attractive, the structure needs attention to ensure that the out-going owner does not end up as a well-funded competitor, and that earn-out clauses cover risks associated with such things as social security, tax, and environmental liabilities. And for those whose approach is just to trust ("I know him. I don't need to do any due diligence!"), it is worth remembering that the confirmation of a deal, by definition, changes the structure of the relationship with the target, as well as the ownership of any underlying liabilities. To maximize the chances of a positive outcome, early commercial due diligence should be deployed to help build the new relationship on solid ground for the long-term, mutual benefit of the parties, and must not be seen as an attempt to pull the rug from under the Chinese party, or simply to hammer out a discount.

Risky Business in Brief: Commercial Due Diligence

- *Set clear objectives and red lines*
- *Address the wider market context*
- *Consider forward-looking issues as well as historic ones*
- *Keep the shortlist open for leverage and options*
- *Use the due diligence process to develop understanding and relationships*

Operational

Once the commercial due diligence requirements have been satisfied, it is time open the lid on the target, and to check that the inner workings match the exterior presentation.

Lui Kam, a partner at Shanghaivest, a Shanghai and Paris-based cross-border investment banking advisory firm, defines the due diligence aims (from an M&A perspective) as helping the principal to[40]:

1. Collect all the important and relevant information required for the investment decision-making.
2. Determine whether the investment is in line with the buy-side company's strategic objectives and principles.
3. Make preliminary valuation of the target company and assess the investment feasibility (various key success factors are considered, while ensuring there are no deal-breaking factors).
4. Avoid or minimize as much as possible the potential investment risks.
5. Facilitate the integration and the transition work post-acquisition.

Kam notes that "the nature and the extent of the due diligence work is generally limited to the information deemed necessary to be investigated," which suggests that it is important to consider (with thanks to Donald Rumsfeld[41]) the "known knowns," but also to seek out the "known unknowns" and to be wary of the remaining "unknown unknowns." On the other side of the coin, Kam warns that "when responding to the investors' requirements, the target company only provides the information it is willing to disclose." Worse still, he notes that the third party carrying out the due diligence generally includes a disclaimer based on an assumption that all the provided information from the target is something along the lines of "comprehensive, complete, sincere, and true, without concealment, alteration or fraudulency."

As a result of the disconnect between the parties some important risk issues can get overlooked, as in Figure 3.1. Kam explains:

In an ideal situation (case 1), both parties consider the same investigation matters at the same time: the buy-side investigates the matters being considered while the target company cooperatively discloses all the related information. Thus, the buy-side would be able to effectively assess and control the occurrence of potential issues and associated risks.

In the worst-case scenario, with insufficient breadth and depth of investigation coverage (case 4), regardless of whether both parties have

		Matters considered by the Target Company		Matters not considered by the Target Company
		Disclosed information	Undisclosed information	Undisclosed information
Matters considered by the Investor	Audited matter	(1) Limited issues and risks	(2) May not be able to dig out some issues Certain level of risks may exist	(2) May not be able to dig out some issues Certain level of risks may exist
	Unaudited matter	(3) Overlooked the audit of some issues Certain level of risks may exist	(4) Potentially significant issues with serious risks	(4) Potentially significant issues with serious risks
Matters not considered by the Investor	Unaudited matter	(3) Overlooked the audit of some issues Certain level of risks may exist	(4) Potentially significant issues with serious risks	(4) Potentially significant issues with serious risks

FIGURE 3.1 Due diligence's inherent issues and potential risks, Shanghaivest

considered the matters being covered by the due diligence or not, when there is undisclosed relevant information associated with the matters not being investigated by the buy-side (whether intentionally or not), potentially significant issues with severe risks may occur after the closing of the transaction.

In other situations (cases 2 and 3), the buy-side does not investigate some matters or the target company does not disclose some relevant information, some issues may also occur with associated risks and consequences.

Overall, when "you don't know what you don't know" matters occur, there is unpredictable exposure to the risks and the consequences. At last, both parties (investors and the target company) may be subject to potential losses. In order to minimize the risk of the unknowns, Kam's recommendations include:

- Perform a preliminary investigation on the accounting firm or the service provider in charge of the due diligence work: they have to know well the target company's businesses and the industry specifics; in addition they must have local practical experience and also understand the local environment and ways of doing businesses.
- Investigate issues comprehensively and in detail (broader scope, longer investigation duration); consider short-, mid- and long-term risks with their direct and indirect consequences.
- In addition to using standardized methods and tools, also apply field research approaches as conducted by Muddy Waters (but take care not to violate Chinese laws, or to be accused of illegally acquiring Chinese companies' or citizens' personal information).
- Carry out in-depth investigation about the target company's internal and external environment (including local government bodies and policies), its history, background, current situation, and future potential.
- Pay as much attention as possible to the employees at all levels (top and middle management, employees, or workers), without forgetting the inter-relationships between the employees or with historical events (including labor disputes, especially as the Chinese government pays a lot of attention to social harmony, and the national labor

law increasingly protects the workers, to the detriment of company owners and management).

The focus on employees is also recommended by PTL Group,[42] who work with investors to set up facilities, and to help turn around troubled operations in China. The wide range of operational conditions across industries and regions in China mean that it can be best to implement a process that begins with the employees as a common factor. Arie Schreier of PTL describes the approach taken to operational audits, noting that the identifiable problems usually do not lie in the financial records (which may look polished even if they are not accurate) but in the human resource records. The wrong people in the wrong positions, with no management oversight or systems in place, are the source of most problems, as good businesses rely on good people. This risk can be spotted quickly by looking at HR records to identify key staff, and checking their CVs and qualifications against the role's responsibilities and salary, and by mapping out the relationships between people. A sales manager that was promoted to general manager despite having no relevant experience might be a concern to investigate but might be found to be reasonable. Where records are lacking, positions are repeatedly turning over, groups of relatives or former colleagues from another firm are found, the red flags demand a deeper dig. Such an approach has helped to establish at various companies that:

- A driver was promoted to sales manager and given a five times salary raise.
- Key positions were held by family and friends of a general manager.
- A Chinese general manager was hired purely because he spoke Dutch.

The records can provide a good starting point for pinpointing operational problems, but they may not tell the whole story, and it is also necessary to speak to as many people as possible from the shop floor to the board room. For example discussions with staff, and a look at the workings of a business, can help to identify when the general manager's assistant is in fact the default manager because she was responsible for all the Chinese communications (i.e., all the important ones).

Foreign investors and managers are often blind to the hidden power and links that reside in the companies they are targeting or trying to manage. In one company of a hundred people, the most powerful figure was a technician who had leverage over the rest of the employees, and could get them all to down tools with a word. In another the "loyal" assistant was found to be manipulating the operations.

Company culture, especially when it is very good or very bad, can be an indicator of operational effectiveness, and it can be obvious from a visit, or picked up on through attention to detail. In one factory Schreier noticed that a warehouse door was left open, and that people were helping themselves to stock without reference to any paperwork. Despite it being noted and relevant instructions sent down the line, nothing changed, and it was clear that leadership and culture needed developing.

In order to get to grips with the reality of an operation (beyond the guided tour), especially when time is relatively limited, it is useful to search out those people who are keen to speak, and also those who have left the company. There is usually a weak link somewhere, that will help let light in on whatever hidden reality may be lurking behind the scenes. This approach is especially useful when a team of several Chinese auditors can be deployed. In addition to carrying out any relevant technical checks, they can divide up the target's team, and remove any untoward controlling influence from the individual discussions.

Outside China most due diligence experts have a good commercial background, and can often "feel" when something is wrong, prompting them to dig around. McKinsey's David Cogman refers to his experience of conducting due diligence on a Chinese manufacturing business which had presented its world-class quality control systems. The operational people on the team were somewhat surprised, and broke off from the official tour to look over the plant's testing lab—only to find dust on all the weights and measures. It had clearly not been used for an extended period, and the QC process was a PowerPoint pipe dream. It took a trained eye to notice, investigate and to identify the gap between presentation and operation. Cogman cautions that "due diligence teams won't see the real problems if they are not really looking, but just box ticking."

The introduction of enterprise resource planning (ERP) systems can help in developing operational transparency, and where there is a lack of such a system additional attention is likely to be needed. At the very least, the workflows and quality processes should be checked on paper as well as in practice. Even if there is no sophisticated system, a lack of the things that make Chinese companies work well, such as hierarchy and structure, probably indicate an underlying problem.

Foreign firms tend to put far too much reliance on their local management, but far too little time and thought into selecting and developing that management, and generally provide too little support or oversight from head office. Schreier would like to see senior management from foreign firms, across all the main functions, get more involved with the set-up and operation of their businesses in China, but there is often surprisingly little engagement. At an overseas China event for CFOs, attended by Schreier, only one of 40 had even visited the market—and that was as a tourist. It is no wonder there is such a gulf of understanding between the assumptions of some foreign headquarters and the reality of their China operations.

Schreier sees many of the same old mistakes being made by newcomers to the market, who are driven by the lack of business at home and hope for better luck elsewhere. In many cases Schreier thinks that these companies would not take the same approach or make the same mistakes at home, or in other, more familiar markets. For some reason, whether urgency, fear of finding a problem, lack of resources, or lack of awareness, too many people take too much unnecessary risk on board when they go to China. For Schreier it is clear that in most cases of failure, the fault usually lies with the foreign business that fails to invest sufficient thought and resource into their China activity. Those risks are usually apparent to those who walk in with open eyes, and can mostly be avoided with local knowledge and careful due diligence.

A more fundamental and strategic risk that he sees for these foreign companies is the emergence of Chinese competition, especially as

Chinese companies "go global" and continue the trend of buying not just resources and real estate, but technology that may make them internationally competitive, and that will very likely help create a killer edge at home. Add to that the fact that it is getting harder for many foreign firms to operate competitively, or to get work visas for foreign staff, in China, and the next three to five years may see significant challenges, followed by a wholesale change in the business environment in the following 10 to 15 years.

SPECIALIST SPOTLIGHT: OPERATIONAL AUDITS: LESSONS FOR INTERNAL CONTROL IN CHINA

Arie Schreier PTL Group[43]

In the past three decades, the technological gap between foreign and local goods provided enough of a competitive advantage to cover a serious lack of operational management and infrastructure in China-based foreign-invested enterprises, but this is no longer the case. China is undergoing an "operational revival" of sorts, and excellence in operational management and infrastructure has become a top priority.

One of the primary drivers for operational audits in China is that language and cultural barriers prevent China-based GMs from reporting accurate and comprehensive information about on-the-ground operations to a company's headquarters. In fact, much of the information reported is not based on multiple sources, but rather a translation of the opinions of one local manager or partner. Furthermore, developing internal "self improvement cycles" requires an openness to constructive criticism and multidisciplinary intervention that is uncommon among traditional Chinese managers.

An operational audit can help to fill the informational void and bridge cultural barriers in China to establish checks and balances and strengthen internal control. Pure financial or legal audits to assess internal control systems are insufficient, as these audits rely on data willingly submitted by the audited company. An operational audit is a key to the accuracy of such data in the first place.

Operational audits can uncover a variety of behaviours that can dramatically affect a company and will likely not be otherwise uncovered, including:

- Employees who signed perfectly legal labour contracts but are not fulfilling their job description (or, even worse, labour contracts for employees who simply do not exist)
- Production losses visible in the factory but not recorded in the books
- Company resource usage recorded in the books that does not happen in real life

Additionally, improved interdepartmental communications and improved management confidence are all by-products of an effective operational audit.

We highlight five lessons (all gained from operational audits) for establishing effective internal controls:

1. Ensure an active and accountable knowledge transfer
2. Invest in recruitment screening
3. Systematize internal processes
4. Keep an eye on distribution channels
5. Prioritize loss prevention

Ensure an Active and Accountable Knowledge Transfer

A key phenomenon in almost every operational audit is a surprising gap in the execution of control flows between a company's homeland operation and China subsidiary.

Logically, when operating far from home, a special effort should be made to increase controls. In fact, in most pre-penetration business plans (especially those of medium-sized companies), an insufficient amount of resources are planned for managerial knowledge transfer and control methodologies.

Often, several HQ departments supervise the planning of a China subsidiary, but the plan's execution is handed to one manager and the active and accountable "matrix" involvement of other managers will diminish as they become passive "report lines."

Good plan execution must consider that the general manager (GM) in China is just as in other countries and that subordinates possess most of the professional know-how. Creating checks and balances all along the chain of command that fit the reality on the ground in China should be done by visiting overseas professionals with the professional weight to make decisions for the organization. Furthermore, these professionals should be held accountable for the quality of the internal control mechanisms they design.

Invest in Recruitment Screening

Managers readily shed blood, sweat, and tears crafting control measures and preventive decision flows, but often spend just a few hours assessing an individual candidate to implement these measures and flows.

For medium-sized companies, a loss of a manager during the first 2–3 years of penetration can be devastating. Since sales in China, especially during penetration, are relationship-oriented rather than brand-oriented, it is all about the manager. Under these game rules, there is no way to underestimate the importance of the initial screening process of a key manager.

Many management failures occur because of a manager's inability to face changes related to operational growth or the scope of their position, an inability to delegate to and develop subordinates, a focus on short-term actions over the big picture, an extreme need for independence related to ego issues, to name a few. These inabilities and tendencies are hard to identify checking a candidate's past record the way most recruiters do, but could be forecasted by professional assessment specialists.

A new tool in China is mass computerized testing suitable for the assessment of large numbers of employees at relatively low cost. These tests are easy to use and include a "credibility test" adapted from security organizations to civil life. The results of such a test will be a major but cost-effective contribution for a job interview, since they point out a candidate's weakness and allow the interviewer to focus his limited time on these. These tests can save a significant amount of search time as well if you use them to prioritize a shortlist of preferred candidates.

Systematize Internal Control Processes

The effort to systematize internal control processes will pay off in the long run in dividends of lowering operational risks.

Return on investment in management systems is not just about numbers, but more about establishing a systematized culture that lends itself to good internal control. Since the local culture is to "look for instructions before doing" rather than to take initiative, a company must create clear plans and make sure there is detailed flow of timely instructions to the relevant employees.

One way of doing just that is using computerized management systems (such as ERP, WMS,[44] and CRM[45]) to structure processes. There are many doubts, especially in smaller companies, about the cost of such a system and especially the trouble of training and adopting the new methodology, but such a project is a chance to restructure the management flows of the company in a very detailed way, delegating many actions to subordinates, interconnecting many decisions flows, and minimizing grey areas.

The same logic exists when a relatively small company implements strategic planning processes such as balanced scorecards and strategic mapping. This enables a new level of coordination and communication between departments and managers who previously tended to wait for instructions to receive enough assurance to become leaders.

While this example may not seem to come directly from the internal control world of "checks and balances," it is essential to encouraging mid-level managers to transmit ideas and initiate their own improving processes—a major step on the way to achieve a structured operation with good internal control.

Keep an Eye on Distribution Channels

While market pressures in China are typical of those around the world, the looser legal environment and the accepted business culture often enables these pressures to have a greater effect in creating unethical business behavior. This is especially true when it comes to distribution channels.

As a company grows, distributors sometimes partner with sales employees to prevent a company from working with other distributors. The sales person only has to say that the new business comes from a "sub distributor" in order to channel the payment flow through "the new partnership," and he becomes a business owner with meaningful earnings from every sale.

The ability to execute such a scam in China is surprisingly easy, largely because most foreign general managers are limited in their contacts with distributors and tend to rely on the sales employee's communications with them. During penetration, fast market expansion by working with a variety of channels can be key to success and such "partnerships" can cripple a company's plans for expansion.

No legal or financial audit can predict the risk of a sales manager that leaves the company holding a large part of the company's business in "his" distribution company, but an operational audit can help managers identify such distribution channel centralization and focus their attention on the sales structure on their segment and the execution of critical NDOs (non-dollar objectives).

Prioritize Loss Prevention

Since preventing losses was traditionally associated with criminal behaviour rather than better management for prevention, in many cases loss prevention is still handled by security personnel, which significantly reduces effectiveness.

Specialist professional service firms can analyze losses across departments, applying loss prevention expertise and equipment to help a company update its managerial flows and reduce losses. With careful planning, a security department can become more of a "profit centre" than a "cost centre."

Final Thoughts

Establishing an effective internal control system requires significant resources and time, but enterprises do not need to approach the challenge in China alone. Another angle to the "operational revival" in China is the increased availability of outsourced professional service solutions.

Service providers can help China enterprises leverage their resources to establish effective operational management and infrastructure across a variety of departments, including back office management, human resources, purchasing, training, logistics, as well as manufacturing.

Risky Business in Brief: Operational Due Diligence

- *Beware of information asymmetry and unknown unknowns*
- *Look at operations instead of financial statements and flashy presentations*
- *Get third-party verification, including suppliers and customers*
- *Focus on employment records and appropriate levels of staff experience*
- *Take company culture and signs of operational stress seriously*

Legal

Legal due diligence is an important part of the process, and helps not only to reveal any toxic legal liabilities and protect against FCPA-type liabilities, but also to help identify and manage important, but non-critical, issues that could have an impact on the structure or value of a deal. However, as with many things in China (or anywhere abroad) it may not be possible, or sensible, to take known and loved processes and check lists from the context in which they normally apply, and to expect them to work well in the un-adapted context of China.

Some of the preliminary legal due diligence processes would ideally have been done at the short-listing and filtering stages of a project, so only a reasonably robust target, which has already been subjected to some level of covert and/or overt investigative commercial and operational due diligence, would make it to this stage. For example, some Chinese companies have been known to use reference to Chinese law in their contract negotiations. Dan Harris, of the law firm Harris Moure,[46] dealt with a US client that was being pressured into an unattractive structure because of what the Chinese side claimed were "legal requirements." The requirements were really just the desired outcome, but anyone relying on a counterpart's word, and without legal knowledge or expert advice, would risk falling into the trap of "legal" negotiations.

Long-time China M&A lawyer, Mark Schaub[47] of the law firm King & Wood Mallesons (KWM[48]), notes that while legal due diligence is needed, it should not be feared, as "good due diligence never kills a good deal." Schaub thinks a good approach in China is to focus on "red flag" due diligence, allowing for rapid identification and reporting of key issues (based on a combination of documentary review and site visits), without the need to wait for every single document (some of which may not be essential) to be received, and every box to be ticked—as that would usually result in impractical and unnecessary delays. In this way the core of the process can be completed in as little as two to three weeks for a typical M&A transaction—rather than have everyone sitting on their hands for five weeks or more, until everything is polished (and everyone frustrated).

A more formal "international" checklist approach might easily get bogged down by virtue of the realities of Chinese business practice— which can include the informal as well as the flexible. The result of the latter approach can sometimes be a very big report (and a very big bill), listing lots of "problems" but lacking the local context which may say that the lack of a building certificate, or insufficient employee housing funds, need not be deal-breakers. These liabilities, which are not uncommon in Chinese companies, can be hard, but not impossible, to clean up. There are no quick-and-easy fixes, and even those who try to restructure the assets to separate them from the liabilities may not find themselves in the clear. Employment liabilities, for example, cannot legally be avoided. A new business can also be complex and time-consuming to establish. Tax issues, if they are not too large, can usually be resolved through price negotiation with the target, following which the venture can move towards compliance.

Just as China differs from other markets, industries and deal structures within China have different issues that need to be accounted for. An experienced firm should be able to tailor the scope of the legal due diligence to match the practical requirements and key risks. Equally, an experienced local lawyer will usually be able to spot a fake document. The main problem for the lawyers is that they do not always have a strong commercial background, so may not be able to spot a tall story in the same way that a spot of initial commercial due diligence might. Perhaps more important, says Schaub, is the ability to spot what is missing from the pile of documents provided—as that might be the key to the hidden risk. David Cogman also emphasizes the need for legal due diligence to go beyond the law (in a manner of speaking), and to encompass commercial reality and the sometimes incomplete and informal nature of things in China.

Before getting into the complex details, an Administration of Industry & Commerce (AIC) records review is recommended. Schaub's experience suggests that "in at least 80 percent of cases you get access to basic records." Most of the rest of the time a summary of details may be provided, but it is rare to get nothing at all. Basic information for companies can usually be found on the local AIC's website. Equally trademarks and patents can be checked online via the China Trade Mark Office (CTMO) of the SAIC and the State Intellectual Property Office (SIPO), respectively. The AIC route may be unglamorous, but it is well worn for good reason. In one of Schaub's cases it was found that the purported owner did not legally own the target business. With that red flag in hand, it was then also found that business did not legally own the land on which it was based. A nasty problem, neatly avoided.

While documentary checks are a core part of the process, they are of limited value unless combined with on-site investigations. In Schaub's words "a paper review is very close to being pointless unless proper field work is done." Without a site visit, one of Schaub's clients may not have found out (until it was too late) that an acid bath treatment facility was actually based in a residential block in the middle of Shenzhen!

KWM recommends a process[49] for legal due diligence that moves from an initial strategic review and planning to site visits, and a three-dimensional review of the target's structure, operations, and obligations:

Understanding of goals: The due diligence process follows an initial discussion with the client to gain an understanding of its industry, project, and intended goal.

Strategy paper: A strategy paper should give a basic legal opinion on:

- The restrictions on the intended business (e.g., whether a wholly owned foreign enterprise can be used and which operational licenses are required);
- The potential advantages of incorporating a new company, including any preferential treatment available to a foreign investor on this basis; and
- Operational requirements.

Preparation for fieldwork: Preparation for fieldwork should involve:

- Liaising with other due diligence teams to minimize disruption to the target's organization and business;
- Providing a list of documents for the target to prepare in advance; and
- Making clear to the potential partner that cooperation with the due diligence process is a precondition of the deal.

Fieldwork: In the case of a Chinese target, due diligence that is confined to data rooms and document review is highly unlikely to result in useful findings for the acquirer, whereas direct research can be remarkably revealing. Ideally, fieldwork should involve:

- Collecting documentation;
- Interviewing members of the target's management, who may be surprisingly frank about the basis of its operations;

- Cross-checking documents and visiting the relevant authorities, including the Real Estate Bureau, the State Administration for Industry and Commerce, the Commission of Foreign Trade and Economic Cooperation and the courts; and
- Meeting stakeholders, including banks, customers and employees.

Contrary to the expectations of many, Chinese business people are often very forthcoming with details of their business dealings during the due diligence process—assuming that a reasonable relationship is in place, and that the approach of the legal due diligence team is one of facilitation rather than incrimination. However, many clients leave the process until too late in the day, potentially upsetting relationships that had started to settle, and making it hard to re-negotiate or walk away from a deal, even when problems are found. Sometimes companies leave it much, much too late, and only retrospectively try to become compliant. One such company, running a profitable but improperly registered operation in China, contacted Dan Harris about becoming compliant. On being told the legal costs would come to around US$10,000 the prospective client went away. A year later, and increasingly nervous, the client returned but again balked at the costs. Finally, three years after the initial concerns were raised, Harris learned that the local employees had taken over the company, and the US owner had been left with nothing "and all because it had never gotten into compliance."

In selecting a firm to conduct legal due diligence, Schaub recommends trying two or three with a good reputation but also looking for individuals with a commercial understanding, and a genuine interest in what the client really wants, and what context is important for them.

SPECIALIST SPOTLIGHT: DUE DILIGENCE DEAL KILLER OR DEAL SAVER?

Mark Schaub, King & Wood Mallesons[50]

For many companies approaching a transaction, due diligence is a tool to confirm compliance or to seek confirmation that their project is not excessively risky. In the context of an acquisition in China, this is the wrong approach. Chinese companies are used to informal arrangements; as a result, non-compliance issues may arise in the fields of employment and social contributions, tax, licensing, and intellectual property, among others. However, if a Chinese company raises no compliance issues, it is almost certainly not a viable option for a project—the target does not need the acquirer and the acquirer is unlikely to be able to afford the target. When properly performed, due diligence should uncover problems and compliance issues, but should go further and provide a plan—including price reductions, corrective measures, and other steps—that allows for successful implementation.

A foreign company's ultimate decision maker may see little immediate opportunity in China, being reluctant to move hastily in a risky market and making full compliance a prerequisite for a deal. However, a visit to China can turn the most cautious chief executive officers into the most overzealous converts. Due diligence plays its part in contextualizing a particular opportunity in the most practical terms.

Risky Business in Brief: Legal Due Diligence

- *Preliminary legal due diligence can be done at an early stage*
- *Flexibility is required to account for informal business practices*
- *Focus on red flags rather than finessing every detail*
- *Commercial as well as legal skills are needed*
- *Purely paper-based legal due diligence is pointless*

Financial

The old cliché requires investigators to "follow the money," and financial due diligence is an important part of the hunt, but in China it cannot be used effectively in isolation. It needs to be used as part of the due diligence triangulation process, and to be tailored to the local environment. Depending on the need, a wide variety of resources and approaches can be utilized, ranging from traditional financial due diligence to complex investigations. Rupert Utley notes some of the variety on offer:

- Financial due diligence: What the M&A and financial advisory teams do in the accounting firms, and which is more of a pre-deal audit with a focus on value of assets and liabilities, balance sheet and P&L analysis, cash flow projections, book of business, future prospects, licensing, claims and warranties, regulatory risk, etc.
- Financial investigation: Including forensic auditing, computer forensics, interviewing, data analysis, asset tracing, following money trails, and general financial detective work. Also off-books investigation, from business intelligence firms, that is similar to integrity and reputation due diligence, background checks, public record sweeps, screening, etc.

One of the challenges for financial due diligence, before any accounts are even looked at, is getting hold of those with the requisite experience— even when using the big, blue chip firms. According to David Cogman, "there are a lot of bright young things in China with great technical skills, but many have been rapidly promoted, and do not have much grounding in commercial operations." The reality is that some of the big firms have seen phenomenal growth and, in the late 2000s, expanded staff at a very rapid rate (at around 20 to 30 per cent in 2006 alone[51]). And some of those staff can soon be lost to private equity and other firms offering very high compensation packages. All this has an impact on training and the ability to deploy the right people. Just as grey hair earns respect in Chinese culture, Cogman believes that a lack of it will be a problem for the big firms for another ten years, and that will have an impact on risk unless businesses adapt and refine their approach to risk management and due diligence. Utley also sees problems with the typical accounting-focused due diligence, and notes that it is often done on a "best efforts" basis, so that "reasonable care" can be proven should a defense be needed at some point. It is quite different from the "no stone left unturned" approach that might be taken on the more investigative side of the due diligence business.

Paul Gillis notes that in the GSK bribery case, "the numbers were not material in the big scheme of things, but the nature of the spending was dynamite." In such a big multinational, while the accounting paperwork would likely have been properly documented and in order, basic financial due diligence may not be able to uncover such hidden schemes. Gillis, like Cogman and Utley, believes that "too many people put too much reliance on the ability of auditors to get to the bottom of what is going on." This is especially true in China where so much business is left informal and undocumented. While keeping weather eye on the financials, Gills suggests there is no substitute for also looking into the eyes of the person in charge, and making a judgment about how much trust can be invested in the relationship.

CASE HISTORY: INSPECTION VS TOURISM EXPENSES

During a compliance review of a manufacturing company, Forensic Risk Alliance[52] reviewed a number of payments made to travel agencies for overseas travel trips. These trips were allegedly related to customers visiting an overseas factory for inspections. However, further review of the supporting documentation indicated that agreements signed with the travel agency contained little to no itinerary detail, and that the agreements did not reference the related end customers or names of the participants. Nor was there any documentation to support the requirement for overseas onsite visits. In cases where itinerary details were provided, numerous expenses that appeared to be tourism charges were noted—they included "sightseeing tickets," "extra entertainment," "5 star cruise ship," and more. It was also noted that some of the end-customers related to these trips were state-owned enterprises (SOEs), and therefore, it is possible that the company may have incurred improper travel and entertainment expenses involving SOE employees, who are considered foreign officials.

Gillis believes that financial due diligence firms often miss what may seem obvious to the trained eye (at least in retrospect). The reason is not simply that the accountants don't know how to do the job, it may be that the client hiring them limits the scope of the due diligence work in order to keep costs down, to speed up the process, or simply to provide a bit of personal insurance cover. Gillis suggests this may be one reason why firms like Caterpillar do not end up suing the accountants for negligence, noting that "they probably did what they were asked to do, but not what they needed to do ... Sometimes, to preserve their reputation and to best serve their clients, firms will just have to say 'no'." Clients also need a reality check, and to accept that they cannot expect to have a smooth ride if they take dangerous shortcuts. In order to reduce the risk of digging a financial hole on the scale of Caterpillar's, there needs to be a balanced approach to financial due diligence that goes well beyond a narrow focus and a shallow dig as part of a box-ticking exercise.

Once the right team is in place Gillis suggests that key issues to be covered in financial due diligence in China include:

- **AIC Records:** Basic financial due diligence should start with a review of State Administration of Industry and Commerce (SAIC) filings. It is a statutory requirement for all companies to make reports to their local AIC office, so it is possible to confirm financial data and details such as a company's "owner of record." Even though there have been concerns over access to, and quality of, the data, the AIC represents the best starting point for financial and shareholder verification.

- **Taxes and Books:** Tax liabilities are among the most common problems faced by those conducting financial due diligence in China. Gillis confirms what many suspect, that Chinese companies often don't pay all the taxes that they should, or do not pay them at the time they should be paid. Many try to avoid some taxes altogether by keeping more than one set of books, or adopt policies to defer the payment of taxes (such as VAT) until cash is actually received, at which point they can also issue a VAT invoice to the customer. There is, as has already been highlighted, also widespread use of fake tax invoices. Any hidden liabilities need to be recognized and dealt with before acquisitions or IPOs, at which point the tax and financial statements will need to match. Gillis notes that most accounting firms operating in China will look for and spot this sort of behavior as a matter of course, but that it can still be hard to catch.

  Historically Chinese businesses have had close relationships with the tax authorities, and at times the relationship has been too close for (regulatory) comfort. However Gillis has seen a dramatic change in the approach of tax officials, not least due to the impact of China's ongoing anti-corruption campaign, but also as they have become more sophisticated. He says "it is now hard to get a lunch appointment with a tax official, as nobody wants to be seen out at a nice restaurant being entertained in case someone thinks they are corrupt, takes a picture on their phone, and posts it online." This view is supported by recent news which shows how the catering sector in China has suffered since the anti-corruption and official austerity campaigns were introduced. The tax authorities have also increased scrutiny of companies across the board and, in the Chinese way that has been demonstrated earlier, have "killed a few chickens to scare the monkeys." It will not have been lost on international businesses that many of the proverbial chickens, like GSK, happen to be foreign firms. Local firms too will be wary, as they think about the future of the monkeys.
- **Trust Loans:** As noted earlier, "shadow banking" is a major issue, and a systemic risk, in China. While many companies, especially in the private sector, struggle to get access to much needed lending from the (state-controlled) banking system, others are putting a lot

of cash into wealth management products that offer high yields, but that also carry high risks, as the products are often based on investments into junk bond real estate and mining deals. Gillis warns that these Trust products are often understood to be guaranteed but are not. The government has already had to step in, and it is a big question as to whether such bailouts will be repeated.

The Trust loan structure presents a big risk in the due diligence process, as the credit risk for companies is frequently hidden. A Chinese company cannot technically lend money to another company, but they often use a bank (which takes a fee, but does not add the loan to its books) as an intermediary to legalize it. The lender registers the transaction as a short-term investment, and the borrower as a short-term liability. The actual risk can vary from low to high, but with interest rates reported to range from around 3.5 per cent to as much as 40 per cent, it is clear that the risk is real, even if it is not always visible. Gillis believes "this is a crisis." It becomes especially dangerous when a company is lending money to its customers so that they can continue buying product. In effect the producer is making a bet, and may be forced to double down until either the customer is able to repay, or the money runs out.

When conducting financial due diligence, a long look at short-term investments is recommended, and a full understanding of the relationship with the counterpart (whether it be guanxi-based, supplier-customer, or other) is needed in order to understand the risk implications.

- **Variable interest entities:** The variable interest entity (VIE) structure is another red flag for investors to watch out for. The risks have been highlighted in a number of cases relating to US-listed Chinese companies. The structure is attractive to the Chinese owner who wants to raise funds, because it is easy to do, and leaves them with a lot of control. For the foreign investor, it provides access to a business that might otherwise be off-limits—but it lies in a grey area and offers little in the way of legal protection.
- **Audits & the big four:** One issue that has been grabbing headlines, and creating uncertainty around financial due diligence in China,

is the role of the Big Four accounting firms in auditing US-listed Chinese companies. The problem arose from conflicting US (disclose information) and Chinese (protect secrets) requirements, and the Big Four's refusal to release Chinese clients' documentation to the US Securities and Exchange Commission (SEC). The result was that the SEC suspended the Big Four's China affiliates from conducting audits on US-listed companies from six months from January 2014 (which was then the subject of an appeal). As Reuters reported in February 2014[53]:

> A suspension could leave dozens of U.S.-traded Chinese companies without an auditor, and could complicate the audits of many U.S. multinational companies that the Chinese audit firms assist with.
>
> The SEC had requested the documents from the accounting firms to aid in its investigation of some of the 130-plus U.S.-traded Chinese companies that have encountered questions about their accounting or disclosure in recent years. But the firms say they can't give the SEC the documents it wants because Chinese law treats such documents akin to "state secrets," and they could be harshly penalized if they cooperate with the SEC without the Chinese government's blessing.

Gillis suspects that a deal will be worked out, but that there remains a risk for the multinationals operating in China, who need the services of the big firms. Small firms may be able to fill the gap, but they may not have the experience required. They will also eventually find themselves in the same position as their big brothers, so simple substitution is not a sustainable option. While the Chinese do not welcome foreign interference in their affairs, accounting or other, the opposing view is that companies invite outside regulation when they list away from home. One possible result is that more companies from China will seek to list in Hong Kong. But the rules may not be attractive there either, as the debate over Alibaba's desire to list with different classes of stock has shown.[54]

- **Corporate Governance:** Corporate governance in China remains generally challenging, and Gillis feels that "many Chinese companies traditionally operate more like sole proprietorships, where the CEO is the emperor with absolute powers of command and control. In that environment boards are often ineffective, and even the 'independent' directors are seldom genuinely independent." As a result it is important to understand the style of leadership, and the relationships between the individuals. Time spent looking at the financial books is important in making a financial judgment, but it will reveal only part of the story. Time also needs to be spent looking at the CEO in the eye, and making a character judgment. This is another example of having to put things in a Chinese context. The background and history of the company and the individual needs to be looked at objectively, and red flags need to be given closer inspection. Old problems may have passed "but tigers do not change their stripes."

Fake receipts or "fapiaos" are the single most common problem in fraudulent accounting in China, in Utley's experience, but there are also omissions, additions, varying interpretations, and other red flags to watch out for. Typically these include overstated sales and asset values, understated liabilities, and evidence of bribery and slush funds. Suwei Jiang also warns to watch for related-party transactions, which can be hidden in shadowy links between a target and its customers or other businesses connected to the owner. The problems can sometimes be spotted in the course of documentary review, but generally it is quite a sophisticated person that can manage a complex fraud, so the type and extent of the problem will often be hidden from areas where the due diligence spotlight is most likely to fall. As a result investigators need to look for the unexpected, to be thorough, and attentive to detail. In some cases Utley suggests it is better to look at 100 per cent of records for 1, 2, or 3 years, than to pick a selection over a longer period.

Cogman recommends that accounts be checked against the whole chain of transaction documents to ascertain whether or not they reflect reality. It is simply not enough to rely on the numbers—as was shown by the likes of Muddy Waters and the accounting frauds they uncovered in Chinese-listed companies. Having big accounting firms involved does not necessarily help unless the right brief is given, and then delivered by the right team. The traditional approach "just looks at the accounts from a certain perspective ... and it comes with a disclaimer" leaving someone else to pick up the loss if the worst-case scenario becomes reality. Utley agrees and notes that, even in cases where there are more than one set of accounts, each set usually relates back to common transactions and assets, and the research has to follow the money back to the origin in order to uncover the most "real" version of reality. Having got to grips with the target's side of the transaction, it is time to investigate the other, supplier, or customer side:

- Does the entity exist?
- Is the payment reasonable in the context of the business?
- Do the shareholders or staff have family or employment links to the target?

Instead of a top-down approach to financial due diligence, starting with the books, an alternative approach (assuming access is approved) is to start with data analysis, using a company's servers as the source, and recovering and crunching large amounts of data. In this way it is possible to comb through all the digital shadows (including deleted and over-written files), and to uncover what the official files may have papered over. In one case this method helped Utley find no less than 12 sets of accounts, across two accounting systems, in a single company (a record perhaps?!).

SPECIALIST SPOTLIGHT: FINANCIAL FRAUD

From Ernst & Young's 12th Global Fraud Survey (China Section)[55]

Risks to be aware of include:

- Imaging software being used to copy the official company chop for reuse in false documentation
- Spreadsheets preloaded with official bank logos and letterhead where users simply enter the transactions and balances they want
- Large quantities of "refurbished" official tax invoices available online, where the amounts and vendor details have been erased

- Internet sites offering point-of-sale credit card machines that can be used to produce card slips as proof of transactions without transmitting the transaction details to the bank

Where appropriate, organizations should also consider:

- Benchmarking acquisition costs or disposal amounts against similar deals
- Independently assessing the business rationale for a sample of high-value or high-volume transactions, such as consulting fees or subsistence expenses
- Conducting follow-up inquiries and/or site visits to major customers and suppliers to verify the amounts, signatories, and authorizations on the relevant documentation

---

Risky Business in Brief: Financial Due Diligence

- *Beware of reliance on the books and disclaimers*
- *Commercial experience is needed on the team*
- *Check the whole transaction chain, not just the numbers*
- *Benchmark findings against industry peers*
- *Beware tax liabilities, off-book loans, fake fapiaos and VIEs*

Compliance

International businesses in China are responding to slower economic growth, and are adjusting their targets to make them more realistic and sustainable. Some are also paying more attention to risk management and compliance issues—from a Chinese, not just an FCPA and Bribery Act perspective. In light of recent compliance problems "there is a strong desire for more predictability and manageability" according to Control Risks' Kent Kendl.

In the aftermath of the GSK case, and with increased FCPA compliance issues, many foreign companies in China have had to turn and look inwards at their controls. In some cases this has meant restructuring operations and cutting down on the use of distributors and third-party intermediaries. But, as David Cogman of McKinsey stresses, there needs to be a balance between managing distributor risk and managing the costs of going direct to market—especially in one as big and diverse as China. Elements of risk will always remain, but they need to be monitored (as do the external conditions) and managed. Cogman cautions that "compliance processes are often a fig leaf. They need people to ensure they work properly, and this requires strong corporate culture as well as training."

compliance processes are often a fig leaf

Compliance, like risk, follows companies across borders and foreign companies working in or with China need to be compliant with major foreign and Chinese laws and regulations (see Table 3.2).

The FCPA is the most common source of compliance headaches from abroad, and China has figured in a number of high-profile FCPA investigations. Avon's long-running case makes a good example, and shows how high the financial impact can be in terms of legal fees as well as penalties. In February 2014, the BBC reported on Avon's FCPA trials and

Table 3.2   Major compliance laws and regulations

Foreign:
Bribery Act (UK)
Dodd-Frank Wall Street Reform and Consumer Protection Act (US)
Foreign Corrupt Practices Act "FCPA" (US)
Sarbanes-Oxley "SOX" (US)
Chinese:
Anti-Unfair Competition Law
Bribery—Supreme Court interpretation 2013
Company Law
PRC Criminal Law
SAIC Interim Provisions on Prohibition of Commercial Bribery

tribulations since allegations of improper payments in China were made in mid-2008, and after investigations were launched by the US Securities and Exchange Commission and Department of Justice in 2011[56]:

> US cosmetics group Avon Products may spend up to $132m (£79m) to resolve allegations it may have bribed officials in China and other countries. The firm has been under investigation for years over possible violations of the US Foreign Corrupt Practices Act … [Avon] has racked up more than $300m in legal and other related costs due to the probe.

The FCPA and the UK Bribery Act are notorious for their extra-territorial application, and China does not like outside "interference." XRG's Hoffmann says that "the Chinese political leadership bristles whenever foreign governments make a public show of being critical of the way things work in China," especially when it involves airing of dirty laundry in public. Hoffmann thinks it obvious that if foreign businesses face legal accusations in foreign venues alleging wrong-doing related to their China operations, China is increasingly likely to react. "The leadership has decided to take an aggressive and assertive stance, and to respond in kind to what might be viewed as foreign legal extraterritoriality." The upshot of this is two-fold: multinational companies accused of a legal breach in Washington or London arising from their activities China are increasingly likely to face legal scrutiny in China as well, and legal proceedings against Chinese interests in foreign venues will increasingly result in retaliatory legal actions against foreign interests in China. These new cross-border, multi-jurisdictional risks are another reason foreign businesses operating in China should strive to ensure operations are clean and compliant.

On the China side, there is also no lack of focus when it comes to fighting corruption, as has been seen from President Xi Jinping's anti-corruption drive. He stated in January 2013 that his government would go after the big fish as well as the small fry, as reported by China Daily[57]:

> We must uphold the fighting of tigers and flies at the same time, resolutely investigating law-breaking cases of leading officials and also earnestly resolving the unhealthy tendencies and corruption problems which happen all around people.

Compliance has obvious commercial as well as legal implications. A 2013 report "Best Practices for Managing Compliance in China"[58] by the US–China Business Council found that 60 per cent of responding companies were more concerned with competition from non-FCPA compliant companies than they were with managing the enforcement of compliance. The Council also found that compliance benefits are underappreciated in China (no surprise, perhaps), require bureaucratic processes, and incur high costs. On the plus side, compliance was seen to help lower operating risks, improve company credibility and branding, and reduce some costs—including gift and entertainment expenses, but also through reducing the use of (potentially non-compliant) distributors. In one case, a US company that had used 300 distributors in China managed to reduce the number to just 70. In the process it increased profit margins by 17 per cent (though there is no mention of sales impact).

The programs also provide a neat explanation to government and other interested parties as to what can and cannot be done. Common, non-compliant requests that were reported included a number that will be familiar to China-watchers:

- Visits to headquarters overseas
- Requests for jobs or internships
- Requests for sponsorship or advertising
- Requests for services from a specified third-party supplier
- Requests for gift cards
- Expectations for gifts (nearly everyone stills sends moon cakes)

Most of these requests are never known to the world at large, as they are dealt with (or rejected) privately. But sometimes, when compliance failures hit the news, they are put under the spotlight. One real-life example of "requests for jobs or internships" came from some of the world's biggest banks, whose hiring of well-connected Chinese employees, some of them related to government officials, brought some high-risk family ties. As reported by Bloomberg in December 2013[59]:

> Goldman Sachs Group Inc. (GS) and Deutsche Bank AG (DBK) are among five Wall Street firms in addition to JPMorgan (JPM) Chase

& Co. whose hiring practices in China are being probed by U.S. regulators, the New York Times reported.

Citigroup Inc. (C), Morgan Stanley and Zurich-based Credit Suisse Group AG (CSGN) also are facing Securities and Exchange Commission investigations … JPMorgan recently gave authorities spreadsheets and e-mails detailing the firm's Sons and Daughters hiring program, according to *The Times*.

U.S. authorities are examining whether JPMorgan violated anti-bribery laws by hiring the children and other relatives of well-connected politicians and clients in China in exchange for having business steered to the firm, a person with knowledge of the investigation said in August. Bloomberg News reported that month that a probe of JPMorgan had uncovered an internal spreadsheet that linked appointments to specific deals.

Now that the risk has made headlines, many more companies will have been prompted to review and make sure their (or their acquisition target's) hiring practices are compliant. Weng Yee Ng of Forensic Risk Alliance, who has worked on FCPA cases in China, suggests that such policies should be fair, transparent, and subject to defined processes, especially when there are links to government entities that may need to be defended.

Reporting structures need to be set up to manage the control and approval processes when risky requests of any type are made, but it is important that these are localized for the situation in China, and that the reporting structures allow for quick and reasonably flexible application of the rules. The need for flexibility was highlighted by a case in which a company required pre-approval from the US for all meetings with Chinese government officials but did not account for the fact that the officials would sometimes make unannounced visits, or that time zones would not play a helpful role. For example, it may be harsh to ban gift-giving when it is so embedded in Chinese culture, so many companies set pre-approved thresholds for the cost of gifts (e.g., RMB200 for a meal with a government official, or an average of RMB354 across those surveyed). The threshold may even vary by city, to account for regional variations in costs and wealth. Others restrict gifts to small items with corporate logos, so that at least the appropriate gesture can be made. Even then, as the Council points out, when the global CEO visits senior leaders, some exceptions to the norm may have to be made.

In addition to internal expenses, there are significant challenges when dealing with crucial suppliers and partners. The report notes that "risk assessments, background checks, and audits are all methods a company can use to evaluate the risk posed by partnership with a third party," and that risk management is handled in a variety of ways:

- Due diligence: "Seventy-seven percent of companies require third parties to go through a due diligence process before signing a contract" and 92 per cent of them use external contractors.
- Training: 26 per cent of companies report providing compliance training to third parties. Reasons for the low figure include the perception that it may amount to interference, and also that it could result in additional liabilities if the training was in some way non-compliant.
- Auditing: This is reported to be a challenge due to the time and manpower required, but is usually included as a clause in third-party contracts, just in case.
- Use of third-party suppliers, and associated compliance risk, can be restricted by using strict approval processes.

Whistleblowing policies were reported by all companies in the survey, but there were also concerns that the Dodd-Frank "bounty programme" that rewards whistleblowers with 10–30 per cent of any financial sanction represented real concerns. There is little doubt that whistleblowing is becoming more common in China, but the policies are not always effectively implemented according to FRA's Ng. The main reasons are:

- Employees are afraid of being reprimanded for flagging up issues.
- Employees treat it as an avenue to lodge their complaints.
- The policy is not properly monitored or dealt with by the compliance team.

However, this does not mean that a policy should not be put in place, according to FRA. The compliance team needs to be provided with appropriate training on how to deal with any issues that are raised. Employees should also be educated, and assured that senior management will look at any allegation seriously. FRA warns that "the existence of a whistleblowing hotline that is not monitored appropriately by management exposes the company to an even greater risk that improper payments may have been reported through that channel but, by taking no action, management is deemed to have "ignored" such reports." Common compliance issues identified by FRA that management should seek to address include:

- Tone at the top
- Gift giving
- Third-party expenses
- Fake fapiao (receipts)

And if implementing a compliance program, the whole process needs careful management. Katherine Peavy of Cross Pacific Partner recalls one case in which a company, while cleaning house, offered staff an amnesty in relation to compliance breaches. When issues were subsequently brought to light it was possible to fix the internal processes, but the company also had to deal with the more difficult issues of US compliance and SOX reporting—something that had not been anticipated. Despite the compliance challenge, it is a job that needs to be done, and Peavy suggests that "those who wear a fig-leaf of compliance are fooling themselves, and will not be able to hide for long."

Forensic Risk Alliance[60] suggests that third-party agents can pose "the single most serious compliance risk for organizations operating in China" and that "an overwhelming majority of recent FCPA charges related to China stem from the use of third parties who have funnelled cash to government officials." The use of third-party intermediaries (TPIs)— agents who engage with government to fulfill a business function on behalf of a company—is therefore considered a key FCPA compliance risk area. Dawn Zhang and Philip Ruan of Greenberg Traurig,[61] in China Law & Practice,[62] note that effective due diligence on TPIs is essential in China, due to the cultural importance of relationships, and as a company can be held responsible for the acts of its TPIs if the company authorizes the act, knows of the act, or deliberately ignores the act. Zhang and Ruan recommend the due diligence process includes:

- Due diligence questionnaire for the TPI, including details of the business, key people associated with the business, and a consent form for the investigation.
- Third-party investigation of online and public sources to confirm the TPI's qualification, reputation and government relationships, and the background and relationships of the TPI's owners and senior staff.
- Additional, discreet third-party investigations into any risk issues identified.

According to Zhang and Ruan, red flags that may trigger further investigation, a new TPI search, or contractual protections, include:

- Misrepresentation of the TPI's or key people's background or qualifications
- Misrepresentation of the TPI's corporate interests
- Key people potentially linked to illegal or unethical activities
- Negative media coverage
- Negative litigation or other reports
  Political or official positions being held by key people
- Relatives of key people holding government or party positions

---

CASE HISTORY: KICKBACK CULTURE

Aggressive targets and generous commissions can work against compliance in any company that does not maintain a sensible balance and a strong corporate culture. In China, where kickbacks remain common it is a particular problem. In one reported case a salesperson for a medical device company was pleased to have received one percent commission on a sale, and did not see it as an issue for concern that an additional three percent of the sale price had been paid to the person in charge of procurement. Indeed, some might think five percent more "normal" (even if some of it round-trips back to the seller). It can take considerable efforts on behalf of an investigator to identify such practices, and to map out how the payments are accounted for.

Luckily, in some cases it is easier. Fraud investigator Rupert Utley recalls a case from the early 2000s in which one well-known German company operating in China had all such payments efficiently recorded in the books as "bribes."

Risky Business in Brief: Compliance Due Diligence

- *Compliance needs to cover foreign as well as Chinese law*
- *Corporate culture and corporate governance require attention*
- *Compliance processes need to align with HR and incentive policies*
- *Due diligence on third parties is highly recommended*
- *Whistleblowing policies can be effective if localized*

Environmental, health, safety and social

Environmental risk in China is as real as the smog that so often covers Beijing and, along with health and safety issues, has become a sensitive political and social issue. The range and scale of environmental problems in China has made the environment a focus of development policy. In 2008 China upgraded the State Environmental Protection Administration (SEPA) to ministry status, creating the Ministry of Environmental Protection (MEP).[63] At the time State Council Secretary-General Hua Jianmin underlined the importance of its role, saying that[64]:

> Environmental protection is the fundamental policy of our country, and is crucial to the existence and development of the Chinese nation

The Environmental Protection Law (EPL) of the People's Republic of China dates back to 1979. ERM, a supplier of environmental due diligence services in China, notes[65] four key policies that have their origin in the law:

- The formation of environmental protection institutions and the definition of their functions
- The definition of environmental liability and set up of the Pollution Charging System
- Environmental impact assessment practices
- "Three Synchronies" system for control of industrial pollution (design, construction, and operation of main facilities need to be accompanied by associated treatment facilities).

Environmental protection in China expanded and developed from the early 1980s, and saw enhanced legislation in the mid-to-late 1990s, according to ERM, including the addition to criminal law of "Crime relating to Endangering the Environment and Resource Protection." In 2013 the importance of the issue was again underlined[66]:

> A number of environmental laws, adopted in the past five years, have helped China to follow a sustainable growth pattern, said Wu Bangguo, the country's top legislator ... in response to severe environmental challenges, the National People's Congress (NPC) Standing Committee enacted the Law on Promoting the Circular Economy and revised several important environmental laws such as the Law on Renewable Energy, the Law on Water and Soil Conservation, and the Law on Promoting Clean Production, Wu said when delivering the work report of the 11th NPC Standing Committee at the first session of the 12th NPC.

The environmental developments are a manifestation of a deeper plan to build a greener and more sustainable economy, including more urban development, reform of state-owned enterprises, control of high-energy and high-polluting industries, and a reduction in reliance on dirty domestic coal and imported energy sources. The message for business was already clear to some, including ERM—who recommended in 2010 that:

> companies cannot afford to take an approach to environmental compliance that is anything but strict, for two reasons: firstly, the legislation is increasingly comprehensive and based on international standards; and secondly, as international companies are perceived to have more resources and experience with environmental issues than domestic firms, they are often subjected to more stringent enforcement.

Despite the clear need for environmental compliance, companies have faced challenges due to the pace of change, inconsistencies in enforcement, and capability gaps in some areas. And it is not just foreign companies that have come under scrutiny, even the previously off-limits, big state-owned enterprises are being pressured into compliance. As the Shanghaiist blog reported in January 2014, the government is taking steps to address the problem, and is putting pressure on companies to improve their environmental performance[67]:

> In a break from its typically transparent-as-wood approach to state data, the Chinese Government has surprised everyone by requiring 15,000 factories—influential state-owned-enterprises included—to issue real-time reports on their air and water emissions.
>
> This decision marks huge progress from just a few years ago, when the government was requesting the U.S. embassy and consulates to cut-off their own pollution reporting. Since then (2009), the government has made gradual steps to improve transparency on pollution statistics; at the start of 2014, 179 cities in China were releasing real-time information on their air quality, according to a report by the Institute of Public and Environmental Affairs (IPE).

The impact for business comes from a fundamental need for environmental protection in an increasingly polluted and crowded China, where investment, growth, and profitability are now having to make way for more balanced and sustainable development. Businesses increasingly need to be proactive and forward-looking in relation to changing policy and regulatory risk, investment in compliance, and management of the environmental and social impact of their operations. Richard Brubaker, founder of Collective Responsibility,[68] and Adjunct Professor of Management, Sustainability, and Responsible Leadership at the China Europe International Business School (CEIBS)[69] in Shanghai, notes that "the question now is whether China's environment can bear the current pace of economic growth any longer." There are a lot of challenges around water, resources, food and energy, and "real questions about the capacity of China's environment going forward." He recommends that companies look beyond mere compliance and instead think "not about the next set of quarterly results, but about 2030, and where they will fit in." He believes that the compliance and sustainability goal posts for foreign (and local) firms are moving quickly. While existing and new facilities may have the right approvals now, in the next 10 to 15 years there is a real risk that businesses with significant energy or water requirements, or with emissions issues, will be moved on or shut down (as was seen around the Beijing Olympics, and as is already happening again to some industries around Beijing). With China's unrelenting push towards urbanization, the pressures will only increase, and the corporate sector will have to adapt.

Piers Touzel, a Partner at ERM in China,[70] confirms that environmental policy in China is firmly in the government plan, and that the current 12th five-year plan (FYP) lays out all China's environmental planning aims, including mass load quotas to restrict the total amount of pollutants that can be released into China's already-challenged air and water. According to a report by China Dialogue,[71] China's 12th five-year plan for the environment included spending of some three trillion RMB, significant expansion of nuclear, hydro and wind and solar power generation, as well as binding targets on resource and environmental protection, including:

• Energy—A 16% cut in energy intensity (energy consumed per unit of GDP), 17% cut in carbon intensity (carbon emitted per unit of GDP) and a boost in non-fossil fuel energy sources to 11.4% of primary energy consumption (it is currently 8.3%).

- Pollution—There is an 8% reduction target for sulphur dioxide and chemical oxygen demand and a 10% reduction target for ammonia nitrogen and nitrogen oxides, the latter of which come mainly from China's dominant coal sector. There will also be a focus on cutting heavy-metal pollution from industry.
- Water—Water intensity (water consumed per unit of value-added industrial output) is set to be cut by 30% by 2015.
- Forestry—China also aims to boost forests by 600 million cubic meters and forest cover to 21.66%.
- Climate—Both carbon taxes and carbon trading have been widely discussed and may be introduced in the next five years, though there is no detailed information on this in the 12th FYP.

With a strong policy focus, Touzel notes that regulation and compliance is also improving, and moving in line with international norms, even if at a slower pace than policy-makers would like. This change is being driven by issues such as air quality in cities, especially in north China, where, according to Touzel, "it is really critical, and has become a political issue" as much as an environmental one. In addition to aligning with the long-term national plan, businesses need to ensure that they comply with the relevant laws, such as the EPL and the 2003 Environmental Impact Assessment Law (EIAL), under which new projects (or significant expansions) are assessed and permits are issued. Those that have potential for "substantial" environmental impact undergo a detailed assessment process, while those that have a "light" or "small" impact can be dealt with by a statement or registration, respectively (see Table 3.3).

Table 3.3   Types of Environmental Impact Assessment Report

Project Type	Project characteristics	Reporting requirement
Category A (Major)	Likely to cause a range of significant negative impacts	Environmental Impact Assessment Report
Category B (Light)	Likely to cause limited significant negative impacts	Environmental Impact Form
Category C (De Minimis)	Not expected to cause significant negative impacts	Environmental Impact Registration Form

Source: With reference to Netherlands Commission for Environmental Assessment, China: http://www.eia.nl/en/countries/as/china/eia

Investors need to be aware of the policy impact on projects, as in some cases it will put an end to a potential acquisition or development well before it comes to detailed due diligence. For example, as Touzel notes, central government environmental policy includes a program of consolidation in energy-hungry and polluting industries. Many small and inefficient steel mills, cement and power plants and mines are being closed down as a result. Facilities under a certain size can be crossed off the target list right at the start of the partner or acquisition selection process, saving both time and money. As regulations tighten, new rules have been introduced, including public reporting and targeting for emissions of fine particulates under 2.5 microns, updated processes for businesses to obtain pollution discharge permits, and for the conduct of environmental impact assessments.

Given the importance of the environment on the national stage, pressure on sustainable development, environmental targets and compliance will only increase. It is therefore an important part of due diligence for any China project—whether for acquisition of a facility where possible historic and future liabilities need to be identified, or for sourcing or sub-contracting, where reputation and brand protection may be critical. For a project's environmental compliance there are various stages of approvals that require permits, all of which should be checked as part of a due diligence process:

- Pre-construction
- Commissioning
- Operating

Once the assessment is completed any rectification (including permitting of any previously unapproved expansion projects) needs to be implemented and then the relevant permits can be issued. The project owner will hold the permits, and should be able to provide them for review during any due diligence process. The assessment requirements vary by industry and by project impact. Assessments and technical evaluations are conducted by expert panels, who then issue a set of recommendations, including approval or amendments to the plan. Depending on the industry and the location, other approvals may also be required, for example safety pre-assessment reports in the petro-chemical sector, as well as hazard or other assessments. In some areas, such as inland and southern provinces there is an additional need for pre-construction permits relating to water and solid waste, as part of special measures to protect against erosion.

An experienced eye can tell an authentic document, but verification has been made easier since January 1, 2014, from when all new Environmental Assessment applications and permits (except those relating to state or business secrets) were made publicly available (previously only limited detail was available). There had been a real risk of false documents being used, and the MEP has taken action against some environmental assessment agencies for deception, falsifying of documents, and other compliance issues. CleanBizAsia reported in November 2013[72] that eight agencies had their license revoked, 24 were penalized, and two received a warning. Fifty-eight technical personnel were also criticized or had their licenses revoked.

Even when a valid permit is issued, care is still needed. The permit may require a certain level of performance, for example, for the quality of waste water discharge, but there may be no requirement for demonstration of compliance, so it will be up to the due diligence team to decide to what extent, and how often, testing should be done. According to Touzel, where an environmental due diligence report states that the compliance was not assessed—rather like the auditor of the accounts who relies on information from the target of the audit—it is wise to be cautious and to check. Not to include testing in the due diligence scope is to invite possible liabilities based on historic non-compliance. In addition to a documentary review of permits, any environmental due diligence (indeed any proper due diligence) should include a site visit, where the physical assets and processes can be checked against the documented ones. For a factory permit that refers to a certain volume of output, a sense check of the size of operation and confirmation of actual output are needed. Two shiny new production lines in an old facility put up against a dusty old permit would suggest further investigation is needed.

Where non-compliance is found Touzel says that it is possible to apply for retrospective approvals, and to ensure that potential liabilities can be cleared up (or the transaction cost reduced) before the ownership of risk is transferred. This policy aims to incentivize businesses to rectify rather than hide their previous non-compliance. Once a deal is done and any land is purchased, the existing liabilities are purchased with it. And the penalties can be severe financially and personally, including jail in the worst instances.

Most international companies, and some of the leading domestic ones, are reported by Touzel to be increasingly proactive in their desire for environmental compliance. In some cases a regular environmental due diligence will suffice, but for more sensitive projects, such as in the extractive or chemical industries, and those which are located close to residential areas or protected land, or which are on collectively owned land, there may be a requirement for a wider environmental, health, safety and social (EHSS) due diligence process. Quite apart from the legal and moral obligations to develop things in the right way, China has NIMBYS[73] just like anywhere else and local residents have not been shy of demonstrating against unwelcome projects, such as a paraxylene (PX) plant that was planned in Kunming by the state-owned China National Petroleum Corporation (CNPC).[74]

In addition to environmental issues, there has been growing concern about health and safety at work in China, at local as well as international companies. A spate of mining accidents focused the attention of state and social media on the human cost of dangerous practices. Beijing-based SynTao,[75] a sustainability consultancy, monitored environmental, social, and corporate governance (ESG) issues in China in 2011 and 2012 (see Figure 3.2), finding that:

> [T]he most pressing ESG issues were found in the social issues category. The category covers topics such as occupational health and safety, welfare and security, labor conditions, and product safety. Overall, both occupational health and safety and product safety received the most alerts for social risks.
>
> Social issues generated 65% of total alerts in 2011 and 63% in 2012. Environmental and governance alerts accounted for 22% and 13% respectively in 2011, and 19% and 18% respectively for 2012.

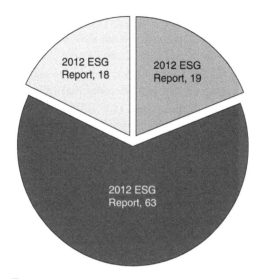

FIGURE 3.2 Distribution of alerts per ESG issue (%), 2012, SynTao

Source: Data from SynTao, 9 August 2013, Environmental, Social & Governance Risks in China: http://www.syntao.com/CSRNews/CSRNews_Show_EN.asp?ID=16358; http://www.syntao.com/Uploads/file/Revealing%20China's%20ESG%20Issues%202012.pdf

Very public accidents at mining companies, such Tonghua Mining in 2013[76] where a number of deaths were initially covered up, and the death of over a thousand miners a year across the country, have resulted in more state and social media attention being placed on working conditions. The supply chains of foreign companies such as Disney,[77] Mattel,[78] Samsung,[79] and Apple have also been subjected to critical analysis of their supply chain conditions and social compliance in China by China Labour Watch[80] (CLW) and others. In Apple's case,[81] despite having conducted 15 "comprehensive audits" of supplier Pegatron's facilities between 2007 and 2013, CLW's independent investigation uncovered environmental and safety issues, unpaid overtime, and poor conditions which Apple had to address. CLW's report "Beyond Foxconn: Deplorable Working Conditions Characterize Apple's Entire Supply Chain,"[82] includes reference to multiple worker suicides and injuries, illegally long hours, and low levels of pay.

The challenge for effective due diligence on these issues is that the targets and associated local interests are not always willing to be transparent, or to reveal what a corporate customer on a planned, formal audit visit might be unhappy to see. CLW's unwelcome and unofficial auditors reported having to deal with factories that called in local police, leading to detention of researchers and confiscation of notes. Among CLW's findings, and of interest to those wanting to conduct effective due diligence, were the following practices[83]:

1. Factories can use dispatched labor to employ people short-term without having to pay severance compensation.
2. Factories can use dispatched labor to shift responsibility for worker injuries onto another party.
3. Factories can use dispatched labor to prevent workers from organizing into unions or establishing democratic management systems.
4. Factories can reduce other forms of worker compensation, and thus their labor costs, by hiring dispatched labor. For instance, when companies contribute to social insurance programs for dispatched workers, they pay a smaller percentage or sometimes do not sign up workers at all.
5. Dispatched workers have no limitation on the amount of overtime that they work. Some have to work more than 150 hours of overtime every month.
6. The dispatching companies often charge the workers a recommendation fee between 20 and 120USD and may also charge a monthly service fee. These fees are quite substantial when compared to the workers' monthly salary.

In order to identify these sorts of risks, a mix of formal and informal, internal and external due diligence measures is required. All those corporate codes of conduct are all too easy for a contractor to break. A useful framework for analysis was provided by The Human Rights and Business Department of the Danish Institute for Human Rights with their 2009 China Business and Social Sustainability Check.[84] The self-assessment includes three sections covering employment practices, community impact and supplier, customer and government relations,

28 questions (see List of Checklists Section), and 245 indicators that help to evaluate a company's compliance.

The EHSS processes can be completed at the same time and normally includes three phases after initial engagement:

Phase1: Desk research, including media and litigation checks, review of project plans, site history, records of sampling reports, and relevant environmental permits.

Phase 2: On-site management and staff interviews (and local stakeholders where necessary), site inspection and any required intrusive investigation and testing, followed by further discussion of findings and agreement on next steps.

Phase 3: Report and recommendations, covering key risk areas, potential liabilities and costs.

Touzel notes that project delivery relies on the application of professional processes by a qualified local team with relevant experience in the sector as well as geographic area. The environmental due diligence team should ideally include people with local knowledge and contacts, awareness of local issues and risks, or even knowledge of local dialects—especially in remote areas where some projects are located.

The benefits of environmental due diligence are not just those of legal compliance and environmental protection. The process can also help quantify the costs of potential liabilities, and can provide important leverage in negotiations.

Risky Business in Brief: Environmental, Health & Safety Due Diligence

- *Environmental issues are sensitive political and social issues*
- *Scrutiny and compliance are increasing*

- *Preliminary environmental review should include reference to industry policies*
- *Permits should be verified with local environmental officials*
- *Testing may be needed, even where a valid permit is in place*

Reputational

Reputational due diligence, or a background check, is used to assess the risks and/or benefits that come with business partners, senior employees (junior ones can be dealt with using employee due diligence processes, outlined in the following section), or other related parties. In China, where the challenges of traditional due diligence mean that less reliance can be placed on legal and financial certainties, it is important to look beyond the documentation, and to understand the history, motivations, aspirations, lifestyle, and family background of potential partners. This sort of analysis is especially important when dealing with the owner or chair of a Chinese business, as the traditional management structure often gives the "big boss" a high degree of control, and as the business often reflects their characteristics and attitudes. McKinsey's David Qiu suggests that[85]:

> We do background checks before we make an investment, especially on the CEOs of private companies. It's really important to find out about their history, notably what entrepreneurs have been doing in the previous 10 to 15 years, perhaps through talking to industry people who have worked with them. Even if an industry looks attractive, we won't invest unless we really like the chief executive. We'd rather be in a mediocre industry where we have confidence in the CEO than be in a great industry where we do not trust the CEO.

Reputation analysis can also be a useful business intelligence tool when seeking to evaluate senior people—whether the aim is for an acquisition, a portfolio investment, the appointment of a distributor, agent or advisor. There are also obvious compliance issues to consider, especially when dealing with TPIs or current or former government officials. Covert or overt checks (or a mix) can be conducted, depending on the status of the relationship and stage of any deal. The sort of things that can usefully be included in a background check, and which can be found using online, media and court searches, along with targeted interviews (and open eyes) include:

• Personal background: If not already disclosed, a bit of research can usually confirm or identify a person's history, including basic facts around identity (aliases are not uncommon), where they are from, their educational and work history, and their family situation and background. These facts help to establish credibility, but also help to define where their guanxi networks may lie, where they may intersect with other key personalities (in one case two key people were found to have links going back to high school), and where additional attention needs to be focused. And while everyone is entitled to a private life, it is good for an investor to know whether a husband and wife team (or a husband with a wife who is a major shareholder) are about to have a divorce.

• History: As history tends to repeat itself, it is worth looking at the educational and professional history, as well as the legal records and media profile, of any individual who may have a significant impact on a business or deal. As well as mapping out the timelines and matching them to significant issues, events or relationships, it is possible to make discreet enquiries of former associates and colleagues who may be able to confirm details, provide background color, or suggest that some areas may be "interesting" to explore further.

• Connections/Guanxi: A big driver for employing senior people and for selecting advisors and representatives in China is guanxi. The hiring of relatives of senior officials by some of the big banks has already been outlined. Not all relationships are corrupt, and having good guanxi with government, in a local area, or within an industry sector can bring significant benefits to a business. A background check can help to confirm whether the target is known to, and has the respect of, relevant peers and officials. It can also confirm, as happened in one case, that some "guanxi merchant" peddling his connection to a former Chinese president was not in fact known to him at all.

• Personality: Understanding the personality, influences, and thought processes of a counterpart, or key decision-maker, can help with planning strategy and anticipating the outcome of key decisions. In one case a review of senior people involved in a major overseas investment by a Chinese firm showed that one had a highly technical approach to analysis, while another was very practical and liked to see things in person. The communications strategy and engagement plan had to account for the differences in approach.

• Motivations: An understanding of motivations helps with understanding of potential risks as well as long-term alignment with the principal's objectives. The profile of someone who is shown to have dedicated themselves to building a world-class brand is quite different from one who is simply focused on listing a company in order to cash in, or one who needs to raise money to pay off gambling debts. Equally, someone with strong political ties or ambitions may become a poor fit for a foreign company that is keen on compliance.

• References: Reputation is an intangible asset that requires verification from third parties who may consider it to be good, bad, or somewhere in between. Formal and informal references can be obtained, and a range of former colleagues, business associates, industry figures, and officials can be approached for feedback on the main areas of interest, and in relation to any red flag issues. For example, if the target of the research is going to be CEO of China for a major multinational, it is good to know that the head of the relevant industry association not only knows of the person, but holds them in high regard.

• Assets and affiliations: The business that is behind the personality may be the main asset they hold, and that would be subject to its own due diligence. But it is also important to understand the impact of any other business interests, especially if there are potential conflicts. Other assets may be hard to identify without formal disclosure by the target, but some soft questioning and background research can usually point to whether there are significant real estate, stock holdings, or overseas interests (e.g., by searching Hong Kong and other relevant company registries) that may seem incompatible with the target's background.

• Lifestyle: Usually more visible than hidden assets, a target's lifestyle can provide clues as to their (legitimate or otherwise) level of wealth as well as their values. Seven different luxury cars, a different high-end watch for every outing, and indiscreet social media postings may be red flags to wrap up and put away.

Reputation is of course partly based on subjective analysis, and results should be considered carefully, and reviewed over time. Even a seemingly "useful" partner can turn out to be a liability in practice. Media entrepreneur Mark Kitto recalls one[86] who:

> to prove how indispensable she was, more than once called in the authorities to investigate our business, then stepped forward to deal with them, thereby proving her usefulness. Every investigation resulted in a financial penalty. That was a bad partner.

SPECIALIST SPOTLIGHT: A DUE DILIGENCE DON'T

Rebecca Palser: The Risk Advisory Group[87]

"On occasion we get asked by our clients if we can tell them how much money the company has in the bank, obtain individuals' personal and family details from copies of their household registration files (hukou), details of telephone calls, text messages or some other equally illegal information. The answer is no.

There are laws which protect certain classes of information in most countries in the world and China is no different. I would be wary of anyone who offers access to information not generally available elsewhere in the world.

The issue in China is one of interpretation. While in all markets laws are subject to interpretation, in China the interpretation is inconsistent and changes regularly and without warning."

Risky Business in Brief: Reputational Due Diligence

- *The power of guanxi networks mean that the key person, not the company, may own the supplier/customer/government relationships*
- *Business owners often have no internal checks or balances so have total control*
- *It is important to understand the motivations of key people*
- *Surface issues can point to deeper problems*
- *Avoid personal data violations*

Employee

As noted earlier in the book, there is a well-documented risk of employees faking their qualifications and inflating their experience. The challenge for anybody hiring an employee in China is to recognize the red flags, and to be able to verify the facts. Anyone who has faked their credentials clearly comes with a moral hazard, and could represent serious risk to an organization once in a position of responsibility.

According to Ludmila Hyklova of the EU SME Centre some risks arise from the fact that there is pressure put on management to develop business quickly, and therefore some issues, such as the quality of the legal framework and labor contracts, are put on hold. In addition, new employees are often hired without proper qualification checks. Hyklova warns that those employees will have access to confidential documents, company know-how, and trade secrets, but may not be trained in how to handle such sensitive information for their own business or future employer—and are often not contractually bound by the sort of non-compete and confidentiality terms that would provide the right sort of protections.

Due diligence into employees or business partners is clearly best done during the pre-contract stage. Depending on the seniority, varying levels of checks—including media, legal, credit, qualifications, experience, and reputational (as noted above)—can be carried out. Nathan Li of Kelly Services[88] in Shanghai notes that "some fake qualifications and employment histories are obvious to an experienced recruiter, and can be identified during initial screening." Initial screening may help filter the more obvious fibs, but further protections are needed. Serious problems come to light only with fact checking, but that is not always easy. Cold calls to a university to ask whether a candidate did actually graduate can often be met with rejection—citing confidentiality, or just a lack of cooperation that may be based on anything from a lack of records to a lack of interest in helping an unknown third party. Even before making a call for verification of qualifications (ideally with a copy of the relevant certificate and a letter of consent in hand), a good look at the document can reap instant rewards. Seth Peterson of the Hong Kong office of Heidrick & Struggles[89] reported one case in which a Chinese candidate for a senior position "did not quite seem the MIT type." Having requested a copy of the relevant qualification, Peterson was surprised to find it included a typo—something that was also not quite MIT!

Other documents that can be requested for verification review include pay slips and business cards. If they cannot be provided, or if the information does not fit, then there is cause for more detailed checks. References can also play a valuable role in candidate screening and evaluation, but it is not enough to rely on one or two, candidate-selected referees, who may not be entirely subjective. In addition to references provided by the candidate, it may be possible to find former colleagues or associates—something done easily via LinkedIn (which is expanding its presence in China[90]). It is also advisable to conduct criminal record checks, which can be obtained from local service providers who can search relevant records.

Not all recruitment and executive search firms have (or if they do have, use) stringent processes. It is a fiercely competitive industry in China, with a full range of multinational, niche and local firms, as well as online businesses such as Zhaopin.com and 51job.com, in operation. Fee levels and standards vary considerably—from as high as 20 to 30 per cent of the annual package at the top end of the market, to as little as 5 or 10 per cent at the bottom—often on a contingency, rather than retained, basis. For a recruitment consultant wanting to make a quick commission on a contingency job, the focus is on placing a candidate quickly, not on finding barriers to the placement. Given that hundreds of people might apply for a single position, only limited time can be spent on filtering, and any sort of verification will have to be saved for the preferred candidate at the end of the process.

A manager seeking to use this sort of service has to weigh the risks carefully, and ensure that checks and balances are in place at some point in the process. It is important to confirm whether the recruitment company does the verification work themselves, or whether it is outsourced to an independent third party. The results can then be looked at in the correct context. At the very least, in-house documentary and reference checks should be used to confirm a general recruitment company's checks to guard against conflicted interests. And it is always worth checking whether such a company has a code of conduct, combined with regular training programs and compliance audits. Peterson notes that a best practice review would include:

- Documentary verification
- Structured interview to test claims made
- 360-degree reference checks with superiors, peers, and subordinates
- At least four checked references, which themselves should be triangulated to ensure consistency

Even after a professionally conducted recruitment and pre-screening process, some 10 to 15 per cent of candidates in China may fail the final due diligence tests. After on-boarding another 10 to 20 per cent of candidates are reported to fall away within six months due to poor performance or fit. Failure to carry out the right sort of due diligence therefore carries significant risk in terms of operations and costs.

Risky Business in Brief: Employee Due Diligence

- *Ensure service providers are professional and aligned with project objectives*
- *Always check references, and include independent sources*
- *Check documents carefully and verify qualifications*
- *Obtain the candidate's consent, and cross-reference findings*
- *Keep a back-up candidate in reserve for due diligence or on-boarding failure*

chapter 4

Putting Due Diligence on the Map

Doing business in China can be a bit of an adventure, especially for those who are moving into uncharted territory. Unfortunately not all adventures have happy endings, and many people have rushed down well-worn paths, ignoring the danger signs, only to find themselves lost and in serious trouble.

Most people would agree that it would be unwise to venture out for a bit of mountain climbing, alone, without a map, torch or supplies, in unforgiving conditions with low visibility, in an area where accidents are frequently reported (crazy—but we read about it every year!). Not everyone uses the same logic when exploring opportunities in China, despite the real risks that might be faced on a personal as well as pro-fessional level. The outward bound adventure is a useful analogy for the China-bound business person. Equipped with the right information and tools—and accompanied by a guide where necessary—managers can plot a safe course for their business in China, and work around the well-known accident hot-spots. What does our intrepid China adventurer need to do in order to "be prepared"? The planning should include:

- Research
- Equipment
- Trial run
- Review & plan

Research

When planning a trip into the unknown, discuss the plan with friends. See if anyone has been there before, or has suggestions or local contacts they can introduce. Likewise, when planning business in China it is a good idea to draw on professional networks, learn from the experiences of others, and start building up contacts. It is worth sitting through the retelling of some of the horror stories, and smug achievements, of those who have gone before.

Figure out what is going to be practical in terms of ability, time, logistics, equipment, and budget. Our business explorer needs to take account of limitations in experience and knowledge, and equip accordingly. How long does it take to get to the starting (let alone the end) point? It is usually longer than anticipated. How hard can it really be? How much?! The cost of everything in China, from professional services to good hotels, is also often higher than visitors expect.

Research may be the most basic risk management tool. Without relevant, up-to-date information it is impossible to make balanced judgements about opportunities, let alone the risks. This is true of the macro environment, as well as the at the project level. There is a risk of "death by data", as anyone who has picked up a copy of the Statistical Yearbook of the People's Republic of China can confirm. An online search for "China risk" is not much better, as 669,000,000 search results on Google can be a bit overwhelming. There are of course plenty of good information sources that, used well, can provide a protective layer of knowledge for anyone who wants to go on the China business journey. The challenge is to be selective, to filter out the noise, and to interpret the findings correctly.

News

News might not always be relevant, but it is important to remain current. As a rule of thumb in China, what was true yesterday may not be true tomorrow. Markets, policies, regulations, and risks can all move quickly. Awareness of current issues and an understanding of historical and cultural context are important. There may be economic risks stemming from slowing of GDP growth (but it may not be in all regions). Or it could be that a sudden cooling of bilateral and business relations due to political arguments (which can result from any number of issues—select as appropriate: islands / spy planes / meetings / shrines / hacks / prizes / other) has an impact on whether billions of dollars are spent on American, European, or Japanese widgets.

In any event, if someone is interested in doing business in or with China, they should keep up to speed with the political and economic news. Publications and news agencies such as *The Economist* (with its regular China section), *the Financial Times*, *the New York Times*, *the Wall Street Journal*, *Reuters*, *the South China Morning Post*, and *Caixin*, have a good range of coverage. It is increasingly easy to stream the publications' China coverage right to a smart phone or computer—for example using Twitter lists. For a flavour of what is available have a daily look at sources such as those in Table 4.1.

In addition to mainstream news outlets, there are many specialist China sources with online Twitter (and other social media) feeds, which focus on business issues. Examples include McKinsey (@McKinseyChina), the US–China Business Council's China Business Review (@CBR_Magazine), and The EU SME Centre (@EUSMECentre). There are also specialist news sources focusing on particular issues, functions, sectors, or locations, such as M&A (@ChinaDeals), IPR (@IPRChina), luxury (@JingDaily), media (@Danwei), and many more.

Table 4.1 Selected China business news feeds

Publication	Twitter Account	Followers '000[1]
Financial Times	@FTChina	90.8
China Real Time	@ChinaRealTime	55.8
Wall Street Journal	@WSJchina	52.5
South China Morning Post	@SCMP_News	33
Reuters	@ReutersChina	13.3
Caixin	@Caixin	8.2
The EIU	@TheEIU_China	5.7

Blogs

Blogging may have had its heyday, but there is a huge database of information and advice available online for those who know where to look. There are a wide range of China business blogs, ranging from the general to the specific (see Table 4.2). Finding and reading a few relevant blogs (most of which can now be followed via social networks), written about practical issues by experienced practitioners, can be a real eye-opener and a useful shortcut to risk identification and even to problem-solving. Some of the more specialist blogs may not generate large audiences, but they might have a very relevant focus for a small group. A couple of hours invested in following sources online can result in years of relevant, and sometimes priceless, news and insights.

Bloggers also tend to be interesting and approachable people, whose online reputation can be easy to determine based on their social media

Table 4.2   Selected China business blogs and Twitter accounts

Blog	Website	Related Twitter Account	Followers '000[2]
Sinocism	sinocism.com	@niubi	25.4
Danwei	danwei.com	@danwei	19
China Business Blog[3]	chinabusinessservices.com/blog	@ChinaBlogTweets	16
China Hearsay	chinahearsay.com	@chinahearsay	9.6
China Law Blog	chinalawblog.com	(China Law Blog LinkedIn Group)	8.2
Silicon Hutong	Siliconhutong.com	@WolfmanChina	6.4
China Briefing Blog	china-briefing.com	@chinabriefing	3.4
All Roads Lead to China	allroadsleadtochina.com	@allroads	1.7
China Solved	chinasolved.com	@chinasolved	1.4
China Accounting Blog	chinaaccountingblog.com	@ProfGillis	1
Quality Inspection Tips	qualityinspection.org	@ranjoran	0.5

footprint, and links to other leading lights in the China business community. Contact with some of the contributors to this book first came through blogging and posting of comments on issues of shared interest. Taking the widely referenced China Law Blog as an example, a sample of posts show that there is topical, actionable advice available on tap:

- "Manufacturing Agreements for China. How Exclusive Agreements Work and Why."
- "Six Great Tips for Doing Business in China. Old School is Today's School."
- "China's Internet and Protecting Your China IP."
- "How to Do a China Joint Venture. Take Your Sweet Time."
- "Forming A WFOE. Make Sure Your Lease Works."

A good way to access the blogging networks, and expand knowledge of specialist subjects, is to work out from one of the established blogs, like China Law Blog, and into their blogroll (recommended) links. Pick and mix until the right volume and balance has been reached. In this way, other specialist blogs can be found, such as these legally focused ones:

- China Hearsay: chinahearsay.com
- China IP Law: chinaiplawyer.com
- China Law & Policy: chinalawandpolicy.com
- China Law Prof Blog: lawprofessors.typepad.com/china_law_prof_blog
- IP Dragon: ipdragon.org

A long a la carte menu of China blogs, that comes ready-made, can be seen on china.alltop.com.

Data

The old saying about "lies, damn lies, and statistics" comes to mind when discussing data in China. There is reported data for just about everything, but it is variable in quality depending on the source, the definitions, the data collection methodology, and its age.

Data is widely available online, and more can be purchased at reasonable cost for most purposes. Frustratingly the data can also be misleading or open to misinterpretation. Still it is essential to do some data collection, to compare sources, and to understand the scale and pace of change in the sector / company / city, or whatever is the topic of study. The mother of all official China data is the National Bureau of Statistics of China: (stats.gov.cn/english), but there are many and varied sources available, from other government departments, news organizations, think tanks, university research centres and more.

Market research

Good old-fashioned market research is invaluable, whether it is bought off-the-shelf, customized and contracted out, or done internally. The internet provides a lot of information, and a bit of dedicated searching can turn up very useful background—sometimes enough, but often just enough to whet the appetite of those who are seeking something specific. Detailed research into almost every topic, sector, and product imaginable can be bought in from a third party if something relatively high-level and generic is required (though beware of publication dates that are no longer fresh). There are endless lists of sector and product reports available online from research companies and aggregators such as:

- MarketResearch.com
- IbisWorld.com
- EuroMonitor.com
- Mintel.com

The costs vary but are not great compared to the cost of repeating the process (or of not knowing the facts), and it is often possible to buy just the sections of a report that are of particular interest. A more expensive, but comprehensive, option is to contract out the research to a firm that has the knowledge and resources to carry out customised, in-market research. The results are tailored and exclusive, and a good supplier can provide real strategic insight and advice. All the collected research can then be used to identify remaining knowledge gaps, and some legwork combined with some sweet-talking on the telephone can usually provide the necessary filler.

Sources

Online news and views, and nicely packaged reports, are all well and good, but it is always advisable to have some trusted human sources to ask for advice, and to test ideas on. For those without an existing China business network, a bit of effort is required—identifying likely people, engaging them, and maintaining a professional relationship. Luckily social networks, especially business ones such as LinkedIn, make it easy to identify good sources, and to make connections.

When heading to a big city like Beijing it should not be too hard to find someone in the large business or diplomatic community who can point in the right direction. But it is likely to be a different story if heading to some of China's second, third, or fourth tier cities, or to some far-flung mining town. By actively building a China-focused, online network, it is amazing how quickly six degrees of separation can be joined up. In urgent need of an English-speaking arbitration lawyer in Dalian, a LinkedIn search turned up a few options. One of them was connected to a number of trusted legal contacts operating in China. An introduction request was sent, and the connection was made. It is an easy and useful process which, if not abused, can be a massive help.

Equipment

Knowledge may be power, but practicalities become important in the field, so it is critical to be properly equipped. Get a guide book (this is a good start!), a detailed map (to define the scope), ample supplies (it always takes longer than planned), and an emergency whistle (in case a rescue is needed).

Guide book

The guide book need not be this one . . . but there is a wealth of information, and some entertaining reading, about every aspect of Chinese business out there. And a book is just the starting point. There are also plenty of experienced guides for hire in China—or for China, just about anywhere you may be. But the best guide may not be the same person as the travelling companion or the good China employee, as objectivity is a valuable commodity on the road.

For anyone seeking to learn from the lessons of the past, some form of guidance, before heading out of the door, is just plain common sense.

Map

A good map is necessary in order to scope out the area, and identify good routes and bad risks. Various options can be considered, depending on how friendly the environment is, how much time is available, whether there are any obstacles to avoid, or difficult ground to cross, along the way. Points of interest can be highlighted, and red flags put down on areas where caution may be needed. Should an accident happen, or a nasty storm blow in, a hasty but safe exit can be planned. By contrast, it is not a good idea to walk into the unknown, without the knowledge of landmarks or awareness of what may lie around the corner.

A map is not of much use if you are heading in the wrong direction, and it is important to stop every now and then, and to triangulate your position with a compass (and, if necessary, to first practice map reading). With the excitement of the trip (and with very limited visibility on a bad smog day), it is easy to get lost and to suddenly find that the low, rather than the high road might have been taken by mistake. A regular western compass might do the job, but consideration should also be given to local risks and characteristics, including unseen forces, in which case a Chinese Feng Shui[4] compass might be needed (see Figure 4.1). In both cases an internal, moral compass should also be packed—and consulted on a regular basis.

Supplies

Treks over difficult ground are hard work, and often take longer than anticipated—especially for those that have not prepared with sufficient training. As a result the need for supplies and resources are usually

FIGURE 4.1 Even equipment can have Chinese characteristics

Source: ©iStock.com, red_green_blue

underestimated. The China adventurer should think long and hard about what to pack, and how much cash to hold in reserve in a safe place. In case of nasty surprises it is essential to be adaptable, and to have a multifunctional toolkit to hand. A sharp knife to cut through red tape or as back-up in a tight spot, a fork (if not chopsticks) for the banquet invitations that might pop up along the way, and a screwdriver to put things back together again should they start to fall apart are a good start.

Finding the way in the dark is something best avoided, especially when passing through an area known to be full of risks. A powerful torch will help to light the way, and to shed light on any shadowy figures that pass by. A torch is also needed to light up those dark areas that are hard to reach, and which are not included on the formal tour agenda. And for anyone that has woken up on a China trip, in the dark, in the middle of the night, with alarm bells going off, a torch is a proven companion! Given the potential for a bumpy ride, and the constant need for enlightenment, several sets of batteries and a spare bulb or two may also be needed.

Emergency whistle

Even the best-planned trips sometimes end up going off-piste, and it is hard to foresee every eventuality. In case planning and resourcefulness are not enough, an emergency back-up plan is a must. For those that choose not to invest in a guide at the start of the process, it is still a good idea to keep the phone number to hand just in case one is needed in a pinch—though it is worth remembering that out-of-hours, emergency calls can be expensive! It is also useful to have a few local friends (or even just contacts) who are aware of the trip, and who can be called on for local support, sanctuary, or at the very least some sympathy, should things go wrong.

Trial run

Important as maps are for trip planning on paper, they are no substitute for the real thing, and a bit of training and a trial run can help test the plan in practice, avoiding nasty surprises later on.

In the business context, it is the physical location and visible operation of a business that can be checked with the help of a site visit and good vantage point. An office in an apartment block, a factory belching smoke, a derelict site, or any number of warning signs can result in a rethinking of the plan. Where obstacles are found, the map and compass can be used to find a way around, get a better look from another vantage point, or turn back and walk away. Sometimes an initial site visit will simply confirm what was expected. Other times red flags will result in a more detailed investigation being carried out.

SPECIALIST SPOTLIGHT: DUE DILIGENCE FIRST

David Dayton, Silk road International[5]

As always, the key to being successful in any work in China is the Due Diligence done BEFORE the project begins—and don't fret if this DD takes longer than the production time of your project itself. It's time well spent.

If you're spending more money than you can afford to lose (or can afford to pay double for the same quantities) then you need to go to China BEFORE you ever start any work or sign any agreements. Visit factories/suppliers' actual facilities, not just their trade-show booth. Go to at least 2–3 different cities as well (and I don't mean three neighbouring cities like Dongguan, Songgang, and Huizhou either). Spread your visit out over multiple provinces and cities so that you can really get a feel for the level of development in the surrounding area (likely where all the sub-suppliers will be located).

A trip to multiple cities in China for 7–10 days can cost less than US$5,000. Compare that with the cost of being 14–30 days late or the cost of shipping incorrect, poorly produced and/or unacceptable product back home.

There are things on the ground that you can never get from Skype, email, photos, and even trade shows—you have to be there to know what it's really like. Spend the money now to be assured that you know what you're dealing with or spend it later on repairs, rejects, late-delivery, and other hassles.

Review and plan

Once all the facts are in, it is important to rest, review, and reassess the plans—and the risks. It is usually not a good idea to race into action before the dust has settled, and the findings are seen in their proper context. The original plan may be perfect, refinements may be needed, or alternatives may need serious consideration.

Lack of review time is a common problem, and can result in shortcuts that lead to dangerous places. Lack of options can also force people to accept unwanted levels of risk, and to follow the plan despite identified problems. Without a Plan B, it is very hard to look at identified problems objectively, and to walk away from a deal.

Lack of options can also force people to accept unwanted levels of risk

Risky Business in Brief: Putting Due Diligence on the Map

- *A plan and the right tools are essential*
- *Time constraints and shortcuts lead to bad places*
- *Multiple sources from different perspectives are needed*
- *Cross-checking is needed to make sure that the details fit together properly*
- *A Plan B is needed for objective judgements to be reached*

chapter 5

Survival Toolkit

Tools of the trade

There are many ways in which due diligence checks can be conducted on a target in China. Usually it makes sense to start with general information gathering, and then to increase the focus on areas of particular interest or where red flags are identified. Research tools that are at the disposal of any manager for no, or limited, costs include:

Online searches

It may seem obvious, but it is remarkable how many people fail to take even this most basic step. Type "XYZ Ltd." and "fraud" into a search engine and, in the worst case scenario, red flags might start popping up right away.

In one memorable case a client's newly hired, foreign trouble-shooter was reported by a kindly whistleblower at a competing firm in China to be suggesting a new fraud, when he was supposed to be clearing up an old one. A quick online search (while hearing all this on the phone from the client's law firm) showed that the guy had been disbarred for stealing client funds, and that he had only recently been released from prison! So much for the risk being in China!! Issues to look for include:

- If there are no results for a company at all, why not? Is the entity a real, commercial operation? The common "China buyer scam," based around enticingly large orders from previously unknown Chinese clients, is often carried out by properly formed companies (in that they have registered with the local Administration of Industry & Commerce)—but they are also often ones that have been set up in the past 3–6 months, and which may have little or no online presence. Others may seem to be listed everywhere, doing everything. In either case, the red flags are very visible.

- Does the company have a website? If not, it's a bit odd. If it does, a quick sense check should throw up any obvious concerns. Is it professional-looking? Does it contain relevant information? Are the pictures obviously stock ones, or do they provide any insight into operations or existing clients? On more than one occasion valuable business intelligence has been found on a company's website pictures (try zooming in on some of those nice-looking photos…).
- Do the address and phone numbers match with other corporate listings, or those on business cards? Does the phone number turn up in searches as being connected to a number of different companies or people?
- Can the site be viewed using online or satellite maps? What else is found in that area or at that address? On a recent case, a number of seemingly unconnected businesses shared links to a common address, and that address turned out to be home to a specialist law firm. With that little piece of knowledge, the pieces of the puzzle suddenly fell into place.
- Are the emails corporate or based on free accounts (though free accounts are still quite widely found in China, they usually warrant a closer look)? Is the site riddled with bad spelling? Is it in Chinese only, even though the company is targeting foreign partners? Try checking Chinese sites (and the Chinese search engine Baidu). With a little help from a Chinese speaker, or even preliminary checks with automated translation software, big problems can be identified at an early stage, or lingering concerns can be given more attention and resources.
- Who owns the company's domain name? Is it the company, its shareholder, an employee, or someone who seems unrelated? In one case, the beneficial owner of a web of companies—who had gone to some considerable effort to hide their corporate links though

off-shore companies, and a team of accountants and lawyers—was identified via a simple search of allwhois.com.

• Do they have a listing on major trading platforms such as Alibaba. com? If they do, are they a premium member? In the case of Alibaba, that would mean that some basic third party due diligence may have already been carried out at some point, and will be visible on the site. Does that information tally with what has been seen elsewhere? If they are not on the main commercial trade platforms, and do not appear to have been at any of the major industry trade shows, why not? More digging may be needed.

• Are there any employees or corporate accounts on social networks like LinkedIn? One prospective employee that was under initial review jumped off the page for having a CV that was a poor fit to his LinkedIn profile. That red flag resulted in a couple of early calls that confirmed he would also be a poor fit for the client's firm.

There are a lot of tell-tale signs that things might be wrong. A little bit of online sleuthing can go a long way, as early negative findings can save a lot of wasted time and resource right at the start of the process. But it is also easy to miss things, or to miss searching for the right terms (including a company's previous name, its subsidiaries, former executives, or other details). A lack of red flags online does not indicate there is no risk, and other tools can still be deployed (as outlined below). But online makes sense as a first action every time.

Site visits

Site visits can play an important role in any due diligence process, whether covert or overt. They provide an opportunity to look beyond the websites and brochures, and to see the bricks and mortar of the factory or office building, as well as the context of the surroundings. If it looks out of place, or abandoned, there is likely to be something wrong. McKinsey's David Cogman recommends "at the very least a drive-by, but ideally multiple, and extended, visits." These visits can, with the right set of eyes, identify indicators of problems—the suggestion of a red flag or the blindingly obvious fail.

Some corporate sounding offices are really just apartments in residential blocks. That might be fine, but it may be a red flag. Some factories boasting impressive staff and production numbers may be idle, belching toxic fumes, or piled high with rejected or returned stock. They may even have a different name, or more than one name, on the gate. Once the location has been confirmed, the comings and goings of staff, customers and products can be observed. Neighbors, delivery drivers, employees, and others can be asked a few questions, and photos can be taken. The sorts of things to look out for include:

- Is the location and building/office suitable for the business?
- Is there more than one business operating at the site?
- Is it open and active, or closed up and dusty?
- Do staff numbers reflect the reported size and scope of the business?
- Are the phones ringing/machines whirring, or is it deathly quiet?
- Are customers and suppliers visible?
- Are staff being active and helpful?
- Do locals know the target, or have insights or concerns?

Sometimes it is hard even to find a site. If a factory cannot be found, that would certainly be a cause for concern … but, with lots of big, new industrial parks, and few up-to-date maps, sometimes it is simply a case of perseverance. This was the case on a recent factory inspection job, where the inspector was only able to locate the factory (on a large industrial estate) on the second visit.

A site visit is something that can be done quickly and easily if the location is local. It can be cursory, or detailed, depending on the aims. If it is in an inconvenient location, help can usually be found in the form of connections, or via the services of a local investigator or inspection company. The results of a visit can vary but should always be seen in the context of local business norms—which only an experienced person will know. As Renaud Anjoran of Sofeast warns,[1] it is easy for the untrained eye to be impressed when on a visit by some good equipment, a few dropped names, and an Alibaba "Gold Supplier" status. In a worst-case scenario it may be found that the business does not exist at the specified address. At that point enough may have been done, and the "opportunity" can be left well alone. More often a visit helps to confirm the reality of physical assets and operating businesses, and provides a bit of background color to paper reports that might otherwise be hard to judge.

SPECIALIST SPOTLIGHT: FACTORY VISITS

Renaud Anjoran, Founder of Sofeast[2]

If you spend time in a factory visit, don't just record the information given to you. Prepare your questions! Asking about private/sensitive issues is a bit rude in China. But I often say that, if a supplier gets offended too easily, he is not familiar with export customer's requirements. And you might have problems down the road with his mentality.

I compiled a list of questions that will allow you to discover a bit more about each manufacturer you meet.

Questions about top management and their priorities

- When was the factory started? What was the previous job/experience of the owner?
- Is the factory profitable? What were its sales last year? And three years ago?
- What is the latest investment made in the factory, and how much did it cost?
- What is the next investment they are planning?

Questions about middle management

- Who will probably follow your order, besides the salesperson? How long have they worked in this factory?
- How many other orders do they follow?
- Where do the line leaders and the in-process QC staff come from? Were they promoted internally, or hired from the outside?

Questions about the workforce

- What proportion of workers came back after the last Chinese New Year?

- What is the employee turnover rate month over month (excluding the new year period)?
- What happens when an operator makes a mistake? Is he/she fined?
- Are operators paid by the number of pieces? Or by the hour?
- Is a part of their compensation based on the team's results, or is it all individual?

Questions about the capacity

- Observe one line that is making about the same product as you intend to purchase. Ask for the output of this one line in one day. Then, based on what you see in a few minutes, calculate whether it makes sense.
- What is the lead time from receipt of all materials/components to full packing?
- What materials/components do they buy? Do they only do the final assembly and packing, or they also make some components?

Questions about the quality management system

- How do they control the incoming components? Can you see it?
- How do they do in-process QC? Can you see it?
- How do they do final QC? Can you see it?
- Do they send samples for testing in a laboratory? Can you see the test result for a production batch that you point out to them?

Questions about certificates and other customers

- Who do they work with? Can they give you references that you can call? Do they work directly with these customers, or through an intermediary?
- Can they show you the latest two purchase orders from a big customer they proudly mentioned to you?

- Can you see their business license, and their export license? Can you take a photo to show your investors?

The last time they made a big mistake regarding product quality and their customer found out about it after shipment, what did they offer as compensation?

See the site with your own eyes
Source: ©iStock.com, Terraxplorer

Company registry records

The State Administration of Industry and Commerce (SAIC; saic.gov.cn) is in charge of business registration and other official company records. Their local offices hold the records of local companies, and are the first (but not only) port of call for due diligence verification.

As noted earlier, in the aftermath of the short-selling scandals relating to US-listed Chinese companies, and some politically sensitive asset investigations, there were some moves to restrict access to AIC records. However recent experience suggests that policy's bark may have been worse than the bite and, while some restrictions are being reported in some AIC offices, access has generally still been available. The sort of restrictions that might be found include access only being provided to locally registered lawyers, limited information availability (especially in relation to financial reports), or access only where the target company has given its consent. The restrictions vary by location and local knowledge is needed to understand local processes, and the most developed areas may not be the most accessible. For example Wuhan is reported to have better access to company records than Shanghai, despite Shanghai's international business focus and more advanced stage of development. As usual in China, there is some uncertainty, and some flexibility, and a likelihood that the policy wind will continue to change in direction and strength.

The contact details of Provincial and Municipality-level offices of the AIC can be found via the Ministry of Industry and Commerce (MOFCOM) website[3] (see Table 5.1). Several, including Beijing, Chongqing, Guangdong, and Jiangsu, have a facility for online company searches (in Chinese), which can provide instant confirmation of details such as a company's business registration number, address, corporate form and status, registered capital, and legal representative.

It is also worth remembering the role that Hong Kong can play in company and key person due diligence. Hong Kong's AIC equivalent also has a searchable database, the Integrated Companies Registry Information System (ICRIS; http://www.icris.cr.gov.hk/csci/), that was saved from AIC-style restrictions, but which does not provide access to financial reports.

Ludmila Hyklova of the EU SME Centre reports that there is a lot of demand for preliminary due diligence from smaller companies looking into potential distributors, partners, or suppliers, and that initial checks typically include the Chinese company's business license, AIC records, and online searches—including, from March 1, 2014, on a new database by the SAIC containing information on companies' "abnormal behaviour" (http://gsxt.saic.gov.cn/zjgs/search/home).

Table 5.1   Provincial AIC websites

Anhui: ahaic.gov.cn	Guizhou: gzaic.org.cn	I. Mongolia: nmgs.gov.cn	Shaanxi: snaic.gov.cn	Tianjin: tjaic.gov.cn
Beijing: baic.gov.cn	Heilongjiang: hljaic.gov.cn	Jiangsu: jsgsj.gov.cn	Shandong: sdaic.gov.cn	Tibet: xzaic.gov.cn
Chongqing: cqgs12315.cn	Hainan: aic. hainan.gov.cn	Jiangxi: jxaic.gov.cn	Shanghai: sgs.gov.cn	Xinjiang: xjaic.gov.cn
Fujian: fjaic.gov.cn	Hunan: hnaic.gov.cn	Jilin: jlgs.gov.cn	Shanxi: snaic.gov.cn	Yunnan: ynaic.gov.cn
Gansu: gsaic.gov.cn	Hebei: hegs.gov.cn	Liaoning: lngs.gov.cn	Shanxi:. sxaic.gov.cn	Zhejiang: gsj. zj.gov.cn/zjaic
Guangdong: gdgs.gov.cn	Henan: haaic.gov.cn	Ningxia: ngsh.gov.cn	Shenyang: sygsj.gov.cn	
Guangxi: gxhd.com.cn	Hubei: egs.gov.cn	Qinghai: qhaic.gov.cn	Sichuan: scaic.gov.cn	

It is usually possible to obtain AIC company records quickly, and at relatively low cost, through an intermediary law firm, or via a credit checking or investigation service (which may have information for some larger companies on file, or even online—which can be helpful when in a hurry). The available data is often very useful, though a caveat is that much of it (such as the accounts) is sourced from the target company's official filings, so may or may not tell the whole story (which may require the reading of two, three, or even more sets of books!). The sort of report generated from the AIC files could include:

- Company name in Chinese (and English where applicable)
- Company registration number
- Legal form
- Registered address
- Contact details
- Date of establishment
- Legal representative
- Shareholders names and holdings
- Changes to shareholdings
- Registered capital
- Paid up capital

- Tax number
- Import/export license status
- Scope of business
- Industrial codes
- Trademark registrations
- Financial reports
- Annual inspection status (see note below)

Using this sort of information it is possible to understand more about the history and credibility of a company, as well as its size and financial strength. With reference to available databases kept by some credit checking firms, it is also possible to check the main financial ratios, to benchmark companies against their industry peers, and to focus attention on any anomalies that may appear in the analysis. Buyers seeking to work with a new supplier, investors, or competitors would be well advised to conduct this sort of search, not just to ascertain the legitimacy of the business, but also to check its strengths and weaknesses from a business intelligence perspective.

Hyklova has pointed out that from March 2014 an amendment to Chinese company law no longer requires companies to undergo an annual inspection. Companies will now self-report via an online system.[4] "How this will work, and what it will mean in terms of terms of data trustworthiness, awaits to be seen," says Hyklova.

Useful questions that can be addressed with the help of AIC records include:

- Do the official records match information provided by the company, including the *exact* name (there may be several related companies with similar names operating from the same location)?
- Does the history and scale of the business fit with the proposed deal?
- What is the financial and operating strength of the company?
- How do the financial results compare to peer-group companies?
- Are the shareholders visible within the operation of the business?
- Do the shareholders or management have any potential conflicts of interest?

- Are there clear red flags?
- Is there any actionable business intelligence?

Documentary checks

As well as using the AIC route, it is possible to obtain a copy of the business license directly from a target company. Assuming it is verified as being authentic and valid, the license will provide details of the company's:

- Registration number
- Company name
- Registered address
- Legal representative
- Registered capital
- Paid-up capital
- Business registration type
- Business scope
- Shareholders
- Registration date
- Period of operation
- Registration authority

In addition to the business license, a target company may require certain additional licenses and permits to conduct its business. These will vary depending on the scope of business but could include an import-export license, manufacturing, distribution, or other official permits. For example, a business dealing in hazardous chemicals may require one or more licenses from the State Administration of Work Safety (SAWS). Depending on whether the chemicals used by the target are specified in the relevant official product catalogues (something that can be checked independently), a production license, safe use license, and/or an operating license may be needed. All such permits and licenses could be subjected to useful examination and verification to ensure that operations are officially in order.

Equally it is possible to independently research and/or cross check the ownership of trade marks via the SAIC (sbcx.saic.gov.cn) and patents via the State Intellectual Property Office (SIPO: english.sipo.gov.cn).

The importance of chops (or seals or stamps) was mentioned earlier, and they form a critical part of any official or contractual document. As such, where there is any doubt, or when all the details need to be confirmed, it is possible to verify their authenticity by conducting a check with the local Public Security Bureau (PSB), where all company chops should be registered. The chop can then be cross-checked with the relevant company's filings and documents to ensure it is the right one, and that it is being used by the authorized, legal representative. If not, there is a problem that will require further investigation.

SPECIALIST SPOTLIGHT: IS THAT A REAL SEAL/CHOP?

Dan Harris & Steve Dickinson from Harris Moure/China Law Blog[5]

Every contract with a Chinese company must be executed by a person with authority and must be chopped by the official company chop/seal. However, there are many types of chops. Which one should be used? How do you know if the chop is real? Here is how you should deal with the situation.

The rules/requirements for chops are different in every city, so there is oftentimes no way to know whether a chop is a proper, legally registered and authorized chop or not, just by looking at it. Given that situation, the Chinese courts have decided that they do not care. That is, so long as the document is chopped with something that purports to be the company chop and so long as the signer is either the legal rep or a person with apparent authority based on the business card of that person, Chinese courts will not invalidate the contract based on a technical argument related to the validity of the chop or the authority of the signer.

Since there are so many kinds of chops, it is best to insist on the standard company round chop using red ink. Some of these chops are numbered and some are not. This varies by district and is not an indicator of validity. The oval chops in black and purple are not common and should be avoided for companies that want to take the cautious approach. Unfortunately, some districts have moved to using these oval chops for reasons that are not clear. Nonetheless, I have never personally dealt with a Chinese company that did not have access to the standard round chop with a star in the middle.

However, the bottom line is that so long as the chop looks authoritative to the average person and so long as the signer has apparent authority, that is all that is required. Due to the variations in practice from district to district regarding company chops, it is usually going to be a waste of effort to do anything more. However, insisting that any legal document be chopped is still required in China, so the basic best practice described above should be used for all China contracts.

The only way to be virtually certain about a Chinese company seal is to do a great deal of in-person due diligence.

For example, you could visit the factory in person, inspect the seal there, and then compare it to review previous contracts executed by the company and provided to you. Or, better yet, you send a Chinese attorney to confirm with the government that the seal that will be used on your contract is actually the company's real seal.

But where the scale of a transaction does not warrant your doing either of these things, we suggest you ask the Chinese party to provide you with the following:

- The signatory's title, in Chinese and English;
- The signatory's name in Chinese characters;
- A scanned copy of the signatory's business card, in Chinese and English (unless you already have a copy);
- A copy of the company's business license, and;
- An explanation as to any variations from the norm (for example, why the "seal" on this document appears nonstandard.

Trademark searches

Whether seeking to invest in or buy from a Chinese company, it is a good idea to confirm whether or not they actually own the trademarks they are using. If seeking to protect a trademark, then early registration is recommended, and a check of existing marks will be needed.

The China Trade Mark Office (CTMO) is the place where all Chinese trade marks are registered. Usefully it has a searchable online database in English, and it is a good place to conduct a preliminary search. A local trade mark agent can make more detailed checks, including for any applications that are in process, but which do not yet appear on the CTMO database. The China Trademark Office website is at: ctmo. gov.cn. A recent, preliminary search for an international fashion brand identified four separate registrations for the name, across several classifications. The brand had been blissfully unaware.

Media review

Much DIY searching can be done online with the help of search engines such as Baidu or Google, but it is a good idea to consider adding a media dimension to the due diligence checks, and to include Chinese media databases and social media. These can be accessed via agencies such as credit checking, research, and investigations firms in China. Key information about company products and services, results, deals and executives, as well as accidents, scandals, and legal actions can be discovered through this process—and might otherwise be missed due to the sheer volume of online responses, because the internet has not been around as long as many target companies, or even because companies might have paid "Black PR" firms to suppress negative stories online. According to TechInAsia[6]:

> Black PR firms provide client companies with both post deletion services to help them escape negative news stories, and some also provide placement for soft ads and hit pieces attacking competitors. The top black PR firms can offer these services even for stories posted to China's most popular news portals.

Litigation records

Litigation checks are also important, but difficult. There is no comprehensive, national record of court rulings in China, so research has to be done. As noted above, scanning of online and media sources is a good start, but if there are significant risks at stake it is necessary to check that there are no legal skeletons in the target's closet.

As a first step, it is possible to tap into the online court record database (www.court.gov.cn/zgcpwsw) that was launched by the Supreme People's Court in November 2013.[7] The site (in Chinese) includes judgment documents from over 3,000 Chinese courts, including provincial High Courts, and the Supreme Court. It covers civil, criminal, and IP cases. It is planned that the scope will be expanded over time. The Supreme Court's database of debtors (http://shixin.court.gov.cn) is another good source.

A systematic check of relevant local court records is the best way of ensuring that serial litigants (and the people most likely to act dishonestly are those that have a history of acting dishonestly) can be avoided. A typical report of a court judgment might look like this:

- Judgment Date: January 8, 2008
- Court: District Court Judgment
- Case Details: XYX County People's Court—(2008) Hang FaZhiZi No.88888
- Judgment: To compensate the plaintiff with reimbursement of RMB88,888

Even if a company has a clean sheet in its local court, it may still have had legal issues elsewhere—whether in other parts of China, or overseas—and it may even have managed to escape legal processes through foul means. In one due diligence case pertaining to a large company in China, there were more than 20 subsidiaries and affiliate companies in 15 provinces. Only two small judgments were found against the target locally—but there were more than 20 media references to legal violations that it had committed, and several detailed online

a three-dimensional approach to data gathering is needed

reports. Ultimately a three-dimensional approach to data gathering is needed to ensure that no major risks are missed.

The reports generally provide the all-clear, or a reason to move on to more specific online and media searches. If major cases are identified, then it is usually a good idea to speak to local lawyers or other contacts who can assist with local investigations.

Credit checks

Credit referencing agencies typically use the data from the AIC as the basis for their ratings, and these can be a snapshot of a company's health. Depending on whether there are any existing causes for concern, and depending on the risk appetite for a particular deal, a positive credit check may be enough for a risk box to be ticked. However a more balanced approach would be to conduct initial checks using some of the other available tools outlined in this section, and to use the credit check as an independent, third-party validation. The credit reports will usually include:

- Key financial ratios
- Scores for financial, operational, and management
- Benchmarking against sector averages
- Credit rating based on a sliding scale, with a note on the associated risk

An additional source is the People's Bank of China's (PBOC) Credit Reference Centre database (www.pbccrc.org.cn). As well as company credit information, which requires a physical application, there is a pilot online database for individual credit verification (https://ipcrs.pbccrc.org.cn).

In cases where pre-deal due diligence has already been carried out, it is good practice to update it on a regular basis, with a focus on any identified red flags. An annual credit check as part of the follow-up process is a sensible consideration, as good risks can go bad, and what was true yesterday may not be so tomorrow.

Reputation checks

While the physical presence of a building or the data on a financial report can help to verify factual information, they do not paint a full picture of a target. Managers are most concerned with avoiding being ripped off by fraudsters, and due diligence processes can usually help identify scams and scammers at the fact-checking stage, and allow for a deeper focus on real business opportunities. Once the basic checks have been done, and things seem to be in order, it may be time to take a more nuanced look at the target, and to move from the realm of objective data analysis into a more subjective one.

Reputation is built over time through interactions with many different stakeholders and, good or bad, it is hard to hide. Sources to tackle could include:

- Government officials
- Former employees
- Customers
- Suppliers
- Competitors
- Chambers of commerce
- Business associations
- Senior industry figures
- Analysts
- Reporters
- Local networks
- Social networks

Not everyone will be willing to speak about everything, but it is very rare to hit a wall of silence when asking sensible questions of people in good faith. Usually it is possible to generate a profile of a company or individual with a few, well-placed questions to a relatively small group of people. Most people will recognize the need for some background checks before doing business, and most people are happy to make some (usually off-the-record) comments to help others do business together—or to help them avoid a terrible mistake. It is good karma they may benefit from another time. It is good to get a mix of interviewees—not all customers, not all angry ex-employees—and to work through some background and open-ended questions before trying to address any specifics. Often interviewees will be willing to suggest (and introduce) others who can provide an opinion.

One of the fears people commonly have about doing reputational checks is that the process of digging will be revealed to the target of the enquiries, that they will be insulted, and that the business relationship will suffer. As a result the more covert research needs to be discreet, and conducted via trusted networks and personal introductions. In other cases it is quite possible to be clear at the expectation-setting stage that the process ("required by" head office, those pesky lawyers, or other remote third party) involves some due diligence being done. It is unlikely to be a problem for someone with nothing to hide, but depending on the circumstances, it may be better to flag it early, rather than to upset an important partner on the eve of signing.

In a place as big as China it can be difficult to find people who know enough about the target to be a useful source, but the nature of Chinese networks and relationships means that there is normally a lot less than six degrees of separation. The popularity of social media networks, such as LinkedIn, makes the process even easier. Anyone with a significant number of contacts in China will find that relevant second- and third-degree connections quickly appear, and that introductions are often offered (and may be repaid at a later date).

References

We have all seen "references available on request" on resumes, but how many have actually made the call to get, and then check, those references? It is always better to control the due diligence process than to let the target drive it—potentially towards friendly references. But it is always useful to have references, whether dealing with a company or a person. The fact that references are offered is meaningless unless action is taken to follow them up. The key is to take the action, review the response, and judge whether the references provided are valid, and whether more checks are needed. Reference checks for employees are most useful when the referee is an easily identifiable corporate or institutional figure, such as a company director or university professor. The most useful, objective outcomes are to confirm:

• Education
• Qualifications
• Employment
• Timelines

If any of the above is not confirmed by the referee, it is likely a foul has been committed, and a red card can usually be waved. References are generally less useful for subjective issues such as capability, as they are self-selected by the target, and it will be beneficial to conduct reputation checks, as noted above.

Pretext enquiries

Another effective form of research is the pretext enquiry. The purpose of such an enquiry can honestly be disclosed as market research, but the client and the reasons behind the research can remain undisclosed. In this way it is often possible to obtain useful information from a target, or associated businesses, about their operations, strategy, pricing and other issues, and to get at least a partial view of on-site conditions.

Cross-checks

Cross-checking is critical, as even when each individual check looks good, sometimes the ingredients do not go well together. It is always important to look at a target in a three-dimensional way, so that not only the public-facing, smiling face is seen. The sort of questions that can be thrown up include:

• Is the registered address different from the business address?
• Are samples sent from the listed factory address, or somewhere else?
• Does the bank account name match the company (or is it a personal one?)
• Are the telephone numbers on business cards and websites the same?
• Are the sales figures credible in light of the staff numbers or factory size?

Risky Business in Brief: Tools of the Trade

- *Conduct initial online and sourced research at an early stage*
- *A wide variety of effective DIY tools are available, some at no, or little, cost*
- *Third party validation of a target's claims can be achieved via official searches*
- *Watch out for and react to red flags rather than expecting to find hard evidence*
- *Where resource constraints and/or red flags require, professionals are on hand*

Due diligence checklists

It is not a good idea to be tied to a restrictive or overly formal checklist when doing due diligence in China, but it is also not sensible to manage the process without a framework. As has been shown, it is useful to build on the experience of others, and to maintain a degree of flexibility, so checking some existing, well-used checklists can be beneficial.

Checklist checks

Experience, and reference to a number of China due diligence checklists (see the List of Lists below), suggests that issues demanding checklist listings attention include:

- Approach: The way in which due diligence is approached has a big impact on the outcome. As has been demonstrated, a narrow focus on financial due diligence and the books can miss the obvious fraud. A good approach should:
  - Be objective and probing: Due diligence that is intended simply to tick a box and confirm the original plan is worse than useless, as it may give a false sense of security. To be effective, preliminary due

diligence should be done early on, the process should probe for (and expect to find) some issues, and back-up options should be maintained to the end of the formal processes so that there is less pressure to cross red lines.

- Take a broad, three-dimensional view, including all the relevant history, context and Chinese characteristics, and look from the top down (for a Beijing perspective), bottom up (for an on-the-ground perspective), and eye-to-eye (with the person on the other side of the negotiating table).
- Ask the right questions: The right answer to the wrong question will increase rather than reduce risk, and an accounting firm may be happy to take a fee to check that numbers on a page add up, even if the numbers bear no relation to reality. Time and thought should be given to setting the right exam question at the outset, and this may require some research and/or support from independent specialists.
- Be independent of the target: Reliance on information and contacts provided by the target increases risks as the target is in control, and can hide or misrepresent things. Information that is provided by the target needs to be independently verified, while introduced contacts may be part of the target's guanxi network.
- Retain responsibility: Delegating responsibility to a junior colleague or unmonitored outside contractor can result in unfortunate errors or, in the worst cases, collusion with the target. The due diligence team should be selected and managed with care.
- Context: Many of the highlighted financial frauds and supply chain problems could have been avoided if due diligence had paid heed to historical cases, and had tested information against commercial reality and the policy agenda. The context should include reference to:
  - The wider market: The due diligence process starts with market research to confirm commercial and policy/regulatory risks and trends in the sector, as well as the target's position and reputation in the market (and to find potential alternatives).
  - Strategy: The business model and strategy of a target can be tested against market conditions and policy direction to ensure it is credible, and can be sustainable even after a deal is done, when compliance, staff, and other costs may increase.

- History: The history of the target and the people who own and run it is more important in China than in many other markets due to the potential impact on assets and compliance of any previous state ownership, sale, or links with officials. History also repeats, and it is relatively easy to check using online and offline tools.
- Competitors, customers, and suppliers: The full picture may not be made clear by the target, so there is no substitute for obtaining feedback from competitors (who may also be targets, and who may have insight into products and services as well as claims of market share), customers (especially the biggest ones, who may or may not be happy, and who may or may not remain post deal), and suppliers (who will know what the target is really buying, and how good they are at paying bills).
- Operations: The focus of company due diligence in China is largely on the operational issues that can be seen and confirmed with the naked eye, rather than with accounts—which may run to 2,3,4, or even 12 sets!). Issues to cover include:
  - Site visits: On-site checks are invaluable as they allow for validation of physical assets, a sense check on the location, a view of the operations, and access to staff. Ideally multiple visits, some extended, can be used. An early visit as part of initial company analysis is highly recommended, as are in-process and pre-shipment inspections when buying goods.
  - Owners: Due to the absolute control enjoyed by founders/owners, and their strong influence over staff, customers, suppliers, and guanxi networks that may include local officials, courts, and tax offices, it is important to know about their background, other business interests, reputation, and motivations.
  - Staff: The books, process, and quality control presentations may be great, but they can be hard to verify. A good starting point for operational due diligence is the staff. Quick checks can ascertain whether they are suitably qualified and paid for the jobs they are doing, whether the appropriate contracts and administrative issues are in order, and whether there are any obvious family ties or conflicts of interest at play. If the staff are unhappy and there

is a high turnover, it is probably a bad sign, and either current or former employees may be happy to explain why.

- Company culture: Culture may be a "soft" issue, but good company culture can energize an operation and can be detected almost as easily as toxic company culture. In a market where compliance and corruption present real risks, and where foreign companies need to be good corporate citizens, a company's culture, ethics, and approach to environmental, health, safety, and social responsibility should be taken into account.

- Financial & legal verification: The underlying assumptions of the accuracy of audited financials, and the certainty provided by legal enforcement, differ in China compared to some other markets. As a result legal and financial due diligence need to be combined with the other forms that have been outlined above. They are of course still needed, and include a focus on:

  - Transactions: Reported income in the books is one thing, and the numbers may add up, but books can easily be cooked for the purpose of a fraud. By following the whole transaction chain it is more likely that the underlying value of a business can be confirmed (or otherwise).

  - Key contracts: Contracts may not be king in China, but they are important. Contracts with main clients and suppliers and with senior staff should be checked by the legal due diligence team to review such matters as confidentiality clauses, lock-in clauses, penalties, and protections (and to ensure that the contracts actually exist).

  - Assets: The ownership of assets, including physical and intellectual property, should be confirmed with reference to verified documents and checks with relevant, third-party official sources. The value of assets may also require an independent view.

  - Licenses: "Regulations, regulations, regulations" ... everything is regulated, even if not always enforced. The existence and validity of business and operating licenses and permits should be confirmed with the target and verified with the relevant government offices, even if that requires approval from the target.

everything is regulated, even if not always enforced

Risky Business in Brief: Checklist Checks

- *Before making a list, check the right questions are being asked*
- *Checklists provide a useful framework but need to be flexible to be practical*
- *Commercial, operational, legal, and financial checks cannot be used in isolation*
- *In the Chinese environment, operations need to be given priority over paper*
- *See sights first hand, and verify documents with third parties*

List of lists

Many organizations have their own due diligence checklists, while others will need to start from scratch. Some useful lists, rules, and recommendations are provided below with thanks to some experienced China due diligence practitioners:

- EU SME Centre: Seven Rules of Due Diligence
- Muddy Waters: Six Rules of China Due Diligence
- China Law Blog: The Seventh Rule
- King & Wood Mallesons: An Acquirer's Checklist
- Fiducia: Seven Rules for a Successful Acquisition
- Danish Institute for Human Rights: The China Business and Social Sustainability Check

EU SME Centre: Seven Rules of Due Diligence[8]

1. **Assess how Chinese companies treat the partner company**
   It is harder for Chinese companies to mislead other Chinese companies, and there is less incentive to do so. So, try to understand how other Chinese companies treat, and are treated by, your potential partner company.

2. **Do not take company introductions at face value**

   It is better to make introductions through your own trusted networks and advisors than through your potential partner company. Any suppliers, competitors, employees, or customers engaged through the partner company may have an agenda benefitting the partner company.

3. **Always ask yourself "Is this too good to be true?"**

   Throughout your due diligence you should remain vigilant.

4. **Scrutinize the company operations**

   Some of the partner company's paperwork you will receive may be inaccurate at best and fraudulent at worst. The best way to know their true identity is through assessing their business operations (due diligence stage 3).

5. **Scrutinize the company's paperwork**

   Always be on the lookout for mistakes such as names of banks, locations, customers, suppliers, logistics, and production amounts (due diligence stage 1 and 2). A mistake may seem honest, but it may also be a crucial clue to the company's legitimacy.

6. **Speak to other stakeholders**

   A multi-level check—have competitors, suppliers, regulators, expected customers, and industry media even heard of the company in the first place and, if so, what is the company's reputation?

7. **Do not delegate**

   Business subordinates may have reason to conspire with the potential partner company, much like the reasons in rule two. Make sure your decisions are based on your own conclusions reached by consulting different independent sources.

Muddy Waters: Six Rules of China Due Diligence[9]

1. **Approach the company as a potential customer does**

   You want to see what the China side customers see. Fraudulent companies have far less confidence that they can fool a Chinese company in their industry than they do about fooling a starched shirt analyst. Moreover, they're usually less willing to take legal risks in their home market (China) than they are in the US. The key to approaching as a potential customer is speaking the trade language and learning the business conventions. If you seem like a waste of time to a salesperson, you won't get far.

2. **Take all company-provided introductions with a grain of salt**
   When companies set up meetings or conversations between you and their suppliers or customers, take them with a grain of salt. The people on the other side owe you no duty to be candid. You have no legal—or even social—recourse to them. In a country where a lot of managers earn less than $500 per month, it's not hard for an unscrupulous company to buy someone's loyalty for the duration of a meeting or phone call. You should instead rely on your own networks to help you understand the company and industry. If you don't have those networks, you unfortunately shouldn't be making investment decisions in China by yourself.

3. **Try to construct your own fraud scenario**
   At some point in evaluating every investment, you should stop and ask yourself how you could have staged everything you've been shown or done with the company. It's good for American investors to practice this mentality because it makes us less credulous. More importantly, this kind of thinking makes clear how surprisingly simple measures (e.g., switching factory signs before you arrive, painting old machinery) can be so effective in fooling the credulous investor.

4. **Forget about the paper. Focus on the operations**
   In today's world where you can buy a competent color printer for less than $200, it's hard to understand why investors place so much faith in bank statements, invoices, and contracts. China's deal-making world abounds with stories of forged bank statements and other documents leading to disastrous deals. Unfortunately, most auditors apply the US audit playbook in China—reviewing and taking documents at face value.

   Big name auditors aren't that well equipped to protect investors against managements who are determined to commit fraud. The following blog does a nice job of emphasizing this point:http://www.terryteo.com/2010/03/how-solid-are-audits-by-reputable-firms.html. Not only is this true in China, but it's been shown to be true in Europe (Parmalat), the US (Enron), and throughout the developing world. Because China's accounting system mandates a large amount of paper invoices, determined management can take advantage of the system to create a daunting blizzard of forged paper that a reputable auditor cannot easily see through.

Instead, you have to look at the operation itself. How much does the output seem to be, how much material is moving into and out of the factory, does the office seem to be a hive of activity, how many employees can you count, what is the square footage of the facilities? These are all basic questions one should concern themselves with during site visits. And it pays to visit two to three (or more) times— a good fraudster can put on a show, but they're unlikely to be able to do it the same way each time. Watch for the subtle differences.

Ultimately if you cannot find a good way to measure the company's sales or productivity (as in the case of a service company), you should think carefully about proceeding with the investment.

5. **Always speak with competitors**

Competitors with real businesses can usually tell you one of two things about a fraudulent competitor—either that it's obscure (sometimes the "competitor" is hearing about the company for the first time) or that they know it's a fraud. Many competitors will be reluctant to speak openly at first about a fraudulent competitor if they know you're a potential investor in the fraudulent company. However, if you're a potential customer who is shopping around for a vendor, it can be a different story.

6. **Do not delegate**

A lot of experienced China investors have stories about subordinates who colluded with a target company to attempt (and sometimes succeed) to defraud the investor. Be attuned to the dichotomy between the investment funds at stake and the income/wealth of the people on whom you rely for judgment.

Clearly the rules of the game are different in China than in the US. There are many solid companies and managements in China. However, unscrupulous people know that most US investors aren't prepared to deal with a full-fledged attempt to defraud them in China. Above and beyond all else, ask questions and never accept an answer at face value.

China Law Blog: The Seventh Rule[10]

Following on from the Muddy Waters list, China Law Blog added a seventh cardinal rule.

Put Documents Under the Microscope

The seventh rule (my added rule) is to put the documents you receive under a microscope because the fraudulent company will nearly always make some mistake in the document. In my career, I have caught the following, all of which threw up massive red flags:

- Company claimed to have a multi-million dollar account at a non-existent bank;
- Company documents showed a subsidiary in the Marshall Islands, yet always spelled the country as Marshal Island. It had no such subsidiary;
- Company claimed to have a branch office in a particular city, yet its documents on that branch office (including supposed government documents) put that city in the wrong province;
- Company claimed to be bringing in twice as much product as physically possible on a particular ship;
- Company claimed to have been shipping out product on a particular ship that did not exist during the first few years when the product was allegedly being shipped;
- Company claimed to have won an IP lawsuit in a country's Supreme Court (they produced the Supreme Court's decision and everything), but there had never been such a case.

King & Wood Mallesons: An Acquirer's Checklist[11]

In order to make a balanced decision about a transaction, an acquirer should have an overview of:

- The target's structure, including: Parties' agreements or board resolutions on amendments to the target's articles of association;

amendments to the shareholder agreement, if any; business licenses; and an itemization of the parties' investment in the increased registered capital;

- The basis of the target's operations, potentially including: Approval from the State Administration of Foreign Exchange; production or product licenses; environmental protection agency approvals; pharmaceutical licenses; certification of tax registration; land use rights and building certificates; and documents relating to equipment and machinery;
- The target's contractual obligations, including: Agreements between the target and its shareholders; loan agreements; major supply and sales contracts; and documentation on product distribution, technology, employees, and accounts receivable; and
- The target's claims and potential liabilities, including: Pending outstanding debts; claims or awards pending with courts or arbitration bodies; discrepancies in audited accounts; and ongoing investigations by government authorities.

- Issues to watch out for in the Chinese legal due diligence context include verification of the basic facts of identity and ownership, as well as issues such as:

- *Land use rights and buildings:* Many Chinese companies operate on the basis of an informal arrangement with local authorities. An apparent owner may see no problem with pursuing a deal even if it has only a short-term, unenforceable buy-back agreement with the local municipal government, which remains the target's actual owner. Land or buildings may be mortgaged and the company may operate on the basis of allocated rather than commercial land use rights.
- *Assets:* In addition to the issue of actual ownership, an assessment of assets must consider customs supervision, production know-how, and third party rights (e.g., mortgage or retention of title).
- *Operational issues:* Acquirers should be aware that state-owned enterprises can obtain licenses for commercial activities that are not open to foreign-invested enterprises; thus, the involvement of a foreign entity may result in licenses being withheld or not renewed. Most companies do not apply Western standards of environmental performance and different standards apply to different enterprises.

- *IP rights:* Although the approach to intellectual property in China has been changing fast in recent years, many Chinese targets value IP rights far less than a typical foreign acquirer would do, and may not even price them into the transaction. However, this approach demonstrates a less than rigorous approach to IP issues and often spells trouble. It is not unknown for a Chinese target to seek to sell technology in which it has no proprietary rights, and trademark and patent registrations must be cross-checked with official records.
- *Employment:* Few Chinese companies can accurately claim to comply perfectly with labor obligations. In one transaction the due diligence report found that 220 of a target's 350 workers were classified as disabled, which enabled the company to take advantage of the value added tax exemption for certain enterprises employing disabled people as more than 50% of their staff. However, none of the employees actually performed work for the company; rather, the company's workers were found to be employed by a third party.

Fiducia: Seven Rules for a Successful Acquisition[12]

If the target company checks out in all of the below indicators, it is in good shape for a future acquisition:

- **Organization & ownership:** Understanding the organizational set-up and profiling key stakeholders and decision-makers will shed light on how the business is run and if it fits with the managing style of your company.
- **Strategy:** Can the company drive sustainable growth? What are their current strategies and more importantly, what were their strategies in the past? These factors can give you a good indication of a company's long term viability.
- **Sales & marketing:** Reviewing distribution set-ups and networks, as well as historic sales performance, is essential to make sure that the company can provide a continued stream of income after the take-over. Sales may be through the roof today, but looking at trends and movements in the company's history can help avoid flukes.
- **Operations:** The reliability of the supply chain is crucial to ensure that there is no chance the operations will fall apart after acquisition.

Full comprehension of how production and inventory management work will give you an idea of how smooth the operations are and if there are any issues that need to be addressed.

- **Staff:** It goes without saying that the quality of the workforce is the cornerstone to a healthy, functioning company. This does not just mean the senior management!
- **Financials:** Yes, thorough financial due diligence follows commercial due diligence, but it still should not be overlooked at this stage. The basic elements should be reviewed to at least rule out the obvious no-no's when it comes to finances. Additionally, any findings here can be used as a framework for financial due diligence later on.
- **Relationships:** The least straightforward yet most important factor in commercial due diligence is investigating the company's external relationships. The complexity of this task is staggering: from assessing the company's reputation in the market to examining the impact it has made on the local community, this research is far more comprehensive than simply doing internal interviews or accessing data. The local community and even the government must be asked for feedback. All of this must be carried out with what we call a "closed approach," meaning that the people in question cannot be made aware of the intention behind the interview in order to obtain the most reliable and unbiased responses.

- **Knowing when to say no**

Recognizing which boxes the target company has to tick in order to give the green light is only half the battle. Clearly defining what the deal breakers are is just as important, especially when doing business in China. For example, what is your tolerance for corruption or environmental negligence? Yes, morally speaking you must be able to draw the line, but also from a macro perspective, the Chinese government has been clamping down on these issues in recent years and we can certainly expect there to be more policies along these lines in the future. China is increasingly conforming to international standards when it comes to business best practices, so turning a blind eye now could result in huge damages not only to your China operations but also to your brand image in general.

• Chinese pitfalls

Beware of the accounting practices of Chinese companies! Not uncommonly, a company may be keeping two or three different books with liabilities unknown to you. They may boost their revenue without having the real numbers to back it up. Digging deeper pays off to avoid having the Chinese government charge you with tax evasion or not paying your social security contributions.

Danish Institute for Human Rights: The China Business and Social Sustainability Check[13]

"The China Business and Social Sustainability Check is a checklist tool designed to assess company policy, procedure and performance in relation to the most essential human rights issues in China. The China Business and Social Sustainability Check contains 28 questions and 245 indicators formulated to help companies evaluate their compliance with various human rights issues in China. These questions and indicators were developed based on the expertise of the Human Rights and Business Department of the Danish Institute for Human Rights, as well as additional research and input from organizations involved in the Human Rights and Business China Project. The China Business and Social Sustainability Check is part of the larger Human Rights Compliance Assessment database, which contains more extensive guidance on all internationally recognized human rights.

The China Business and Social Sustainability Check covers three main topic areas:

1. Employment practices—the rights of individuals employed by the company or seeking employment with the company. This topic area covers only those directly employed by the company.
2. Community impact—the rights of individuals residing in communities (as defined by political, cultural, or geographic boundaries) that are affected by company activities. This topic area covers only those communities directly affected by company operations.

3. Supplier, customer, and government relations—due diligence with regard to business associates and other stakeholders whose actions may lead to company complicity, as well as users of company products and services. The scope of this area extends to the outermost limits of the company's sphere of influence.

A. *Employment Practices*
   No. 1: Hours of Work
   No. 2: Living Wage
   No. 3: Procedures on Salary and Other Payments
   No. 4: Leave and Holiday
   No. 5: Workplace Health and Safety Standards
   No. 6: Training and Protective Gear
   No. 7: Labour Contracts
   No. 8: Equal Treatment
   No. 9: Migrant Workers
   No. 10: Minimum Age Standards
   No. 11: Young Workers and Worst Forms of Child Labour
   No. 12: Freedom of Movement and Choice in Work
   No. 17: Internal Grievance Mechanisms
   No. 18: Company-provided Dining Facilities
   No. 19: Company-provided Housing Facilities

B. *Community Impact*
   No. 20: Consulting Legal and Customary Owners of Land
   No. 21: Relocations and Usage of Company Land
   No. 22: Environmental Health
   No. 23: Environmental Safety
   No. 24: External Grievance Mechanisms

C. *Supplier, Customer, and Government Relations*
   No. 25: Supply Chain Management
   No. 26: Recruitment Agencies
   No. 27: Company Products and Consumer Protection
   No. 28: Corruption and Bribery"

Risky Business in Brief: List of Lists

- *Ask yourself "is this too good to be true?" and expect to find some issues*
- *Understand the organization structure and owners' background*
- *Focus on the operations, and don't ignore health, safety, and the environment*
- *Put documents under the microscope, and verify with third parties*
- *Check key contracts with clients and stakeholders, don't just rely on accounts*

6

Emergency Services

When looking for and evaluating risks, there is always a risk that an untrained eye could miss an important detail, or that a red flag, when spotted, requires specialist services and/or additional resources to come in, investigate, and help to find a way through to a successful resolution. When a due diligence alarm goes off, the support of an army of emergency services is at hand. The service suppliers range from risk managers and investigators to accountants and lawyers, and include large and small, local and international firms. The right fit of service will depend on the type and scope of issues to be addressed, the level of sensitivity, the internal skills, capacity, and budget that is already available, and the required timeframe for delivery.

Of course, it may seem hard to do due diligence on the providers of due diligence services, but the principles are the same. Business networks and recommendations can help to build a shortlist, and then some of the DIY tools can be used to qualify them before making a direct approach. A common reason for rushing the identification and selection process is that there is already a live crisis that needs to be managed. As China demonstrably involves risk, and as due diligence is most useful when it is proactive and early-stage, one option is to take a small, non-critical project, engage the relevant due diligence services, and evaluate the benefits. An understanding of the process can be developed and, in addition to business intelligence obtained or business risk identified, a potential supplier can be qualified (or disqualified) for a future emergency. Issues to bear in mind when selecting and dealing with due diligence service suppliers include:

- Confidentiality: For sensitive issues a sensitive approach should be taken to communications and division of labour.
- Reputation and recommendation: Leverage networks for advice.
- Track record: Check credentials, conflicts of interest, and case history.
- Red flags: Note if inappropriate activities are referenced or confidences disclosed.
- Key contact: Understand who the contact person is, what role they will play in any project, and who will be doing the work.
- Resources: Consider sector as well as functional expertise, as some industries have specific risks and working practices that need to be understood.
- Location: Local networks and knowledge are important. Multiple locations may need to be covered, and more than one provider may be needed.

Once a service provider is in place, service commissioning can begin. As due diligence projects can be like pieces of string, it is hard to know how long or how costly they will be (especially if red flags are found and require further investigation). However, there are a range of services that can be easily defined and delivered within one to three weeks on a fixed-cost basis, ranging from a few hundred to a few thousand dollars, including:

- Credit checks: Often available online or on short notice.
- Company analysis reports: Combining AIC records with legal, media checks, site visits, and sourced interviews.
- Reputation checks: Including online media and legal checks with targeted interviews.
- Factory audits: Health, safety, environmental, and other issues can be checked.

- In process and pre-shipment inspections: Providing testing and photographic checks based on agreed criteria.

The risk management industry, like most in China, is competitive, but costs are increasing in line with salaries and overheads, and with the increasing pressure of compliance.

Consultants

General consultants

Consultants come in all shapes and sizes, from the big multinationals to the niche advisors. The big companies are well represented in the major cities such as Beijing, Shanghai, and Hong Kong, and some that are further afield. There are also plenty of small- and mid-sized firms, who may have a footprint in less popular places and/or who may be staffed by people with experience in one of the bigger firms. The list of consultants is a very long one, as they cover different functions, sectors, and locations, but many can be found with reference to business networks, local chambers of commerce, and other associations. English-language sources to scan for relevant members and/or approved consultants include the following (many countries have comparable organisations and listings):

- American Chamber of Commerce: www.amchamchina.org
- British Chamber of Commerce: www.britishchamber.cn
- European Chamber of Commerce: www.euccc.com.cn/en
- EU SME Centre: www.eusmecentre.org.cn
- EU IPR Helpdesk: www.iprhelpdesk.eu
- The China Advisors Network: www.china-advisers-network.com
- The China Business Network: www.thechinabusinessnetwork.com
- The China–Britain Business Council: www.http://www.cbbc.org
- The US–China Business Council: www.uschina.org

Investigations and risk management

The investigations industry ranges from the big international players such as Kroll and Control Risks, through to smaller, niche players and local "fixers." The best operators have a mix of good people and systems, as well as sensible controls and boundaries. At the other end of the scale there are others who will do "whatever it takes" and who risk falling foul of the law. There is not yet any formal industry association for the investigations sector in China, though some attempts have been made. A number of options can be found with reference to the sources noted above.

Fees vary greatly depending on the provider and type of service, but fees often fall into the US$5,000 to US$20,000 range for due diligence investigations, while confirmation of basic data, credit and legal checks, or on-site inspections can range upwards from several hundred US dollars.

Environmental consultants

There are a variety of environmental due diligence suppliers, including local and international firms, and ranging from the small to the multinational. International companies tend to use the services of the international service providers, as they tend to be operationally aligned, have often worked together in other markets, and have the required levels of liability protection. Many local service providers have historically had links to government, but the Environmental Protection Bureaus were forced to spin off their commercial operations in an effort to reduce obvious conflicts of interest. For environmental impact assessments, the consultant should be certified by the Ministry of Environmental Protection at local or national level, depending on the category of project in question.

Compared to the potential liabilities, the cost of services, even from the big international providers, need not be high. The scale of costs for initial desk research can range up from around US$5,000 for a small project, though the large scale of many projects that need significant environmental checks can bring the costs to US$50,000–US$100,000 or more.

Even a small investment can highlight risk
Source: Image by the author, as seen on the road at West Hill, Kunming, 2013

Lawyers

With so much interest—and risk—in China, it is no surprise that there is a well-served legal market. While the big international firms are in China (there are over 200 representative offices of foreign law firms licensed by the Ministry of Justice (MOJ) in China[1]) alongside a variety of local ones, David Cogman of McKinsey notes that some are more commercial than others. He explains that many international firms use a preferred global law firm—which will usually have a local partner or affiliate (perhaps a tier two or three local firm) in China, and which may not be the best for every eventuality. While Cogman does not doubt the professionalism of the big global firms, he suggests tailoring the legal due diligence team to the local environment, and looking at ways to ensure a good balance of local team content and commercial experience. Despite the challenging local conditions, and the well-documented problems associated with many deals—some of which were covered earlier—clients can be conservative, and reluctant to take advice and to change their processes. In such cases the results may be less than optimal.

The variety on offer is indicated by the international and domestic winners of the China Law & Practice Awards 2013[2]:

- Banking & Finance: Allan & Overy; Concord & Partners
- Capital Markets: Davis Polk & Wardwell; Zhong Lun
- M&A: Freshfields Bruckhaus Deringer; Jun He
- Private Equity: Skadden Arps Slate Meagher & Flom; Fangda Partners
- Projects, Energy & Infrastructure: Vinson & Elkins; Guantao

Even those foreign firms without an office in China will often be part of one of the many international legal networks, providing them arms-length representation in the market through a partner. Major networks with China representation include:

- ALFA International: www.alfainternational.com
- Lex Mundi: www.lexmundi.com
- Meritas: www.meritas.org
- TAGLaw: www.taglaw.com
- TerraLex: www.terralex.org

In addition the legal listings sites have done a lot of work to research and qualify local law firms in the market. The sites include:

- Chambers & Partners: www.chambersandpartners.com/guide/global /2/60/1
- IFLR: www.iflr1000.com/pdfs/Directories/34/China-xtended4web. qxd.pdf
- Legal 500 directory: www.legal500.com/c/china/directory

Accountants

The *Financial Times*[3] has noted that "The Big Four's share of the fees garnered by the top 100 Chinese firms peaked at 55 per cent in 2007 and had slipped to 36 per cent in 2011." Paul Gillis has reported that they were down to 34 per cent by 2013.[4] The "big four" are no longer the biggest four in China, according to the Chinese Institute of Certified Public Accountants,[5] who put local firm Ruihua at number three, ahead of Ernst & Young, while KPMG came in at number six. The big four are well established in the market, but local firms were reported to make up half of the top 10 in 2013[6]:

- PwC
- Deloitte
- Ruihua
- E&Y
- BDO
- KPMG
- Daxin
- Tianjian
- Shinewing
- Dahua

Mid-tier firms and the leading international accounting alliances are increasingly challenging the big firms, often working in affiliation with local representation in China. These networks include[7]:

- Appleton Group Alliance: www.tiagnet.com
- Geneva Group International: www.ggi.com
- Leading Edge Alliance: www.leadingedgealliance.com
- PKF International: www.pkf.com
- Praxity AISBL: www.praxity.com

Some accounting firms are reported to be keen to keep their big clients happy, and to make a profit in what is a very competitive market—even when they take on a fixed-price contract. When retaining a firm to do financial due diligence, real thought needs to be given to the structure and to the downside risk of the terms of engagement—not just to the short term and the level of fees.

Risky Business in Brief: Emergency Services

- *A range of competitive local and international service firms are available*
- *International reputation needs to be balanced with local capability and footprint*
- *Suppliers can be identified via chambers of commerce and other networks*
- *Get to know and test service providers before they are needed in an emergency*
- *There is a downside associated with fixed-fee contracts—balance is needed*

7

The Good, the Bad, and the Ugly

Some real-life examples of past cases are proof of the variety of risks that have to be addressed, the effectiveness of the tools that can be deployed, and the benefits that due diligence can bring. When conducted at the start of the process it can strengthen the business position, even when no major threat is identified ("the good"). In some cases bad things are found, but often in time to put them right ("the bad"). Sadly, some cases are all about post-impact damage limitation, often because no proper due diligence was done at the outset ("the ugly").

The Good

Good practices generally provide good results. Due diligence need not be time-consuming or expensive but can be appropriate to the deal size and risk profile. The Good examples below focus on the impact of:

- The commercial context
- Basic due diligence and business intelligence
- Early application of commercial due diligence on multiple targets
- Ethical compliance checks that get under the surface

The whole truth

One legal due diligence case involved a junior lawyer who conducted the essential on-site due diligence, and prepared a perfectly good-looking report. An interesting element that was lacking was an interview with the General Manager. Asked why this was, the lawyer replied that the GM was not there. Further prompting revealed he was in prison for murder. It turned out that one of the feuding shareholders of the acquisition target had tried to have him assassinated, but that he had killed the would-be assassin.

As the criminal case was closed, and diligent though the lawyer was, he had thought it was not relevant to include in the legal due diligence report. The client, needless to say, was glad to know the facts that lay beyond the ticked boxes!

- Toolkit: Site visit; management interviews; commercial context.
- Conclusion: It is important to ensure that the due diligence team gets on site, has a commercial background, understands the principal's concerns, and is able to judge the context.

Intelligent business

A foreign client, sourcing from China for the first time, was seeking to buy Chinese vehicles for export and required basic due diligence on the identified supplier. The due diligence was completed in about a week, and included checking of AIC records, the company's financial position, media and litigation checks, as well as a covert site visit and discreet reputational enquires. The client was pleased to find that the supplier ticked all the basic due diligence boxes. They were also interested to see that analysis of the financials showed slowing business growth, and increasing levels of inventory. A bit of research into the business's operations found that the supplier had set export development as a core part of their growth plan. The client was then able to enter the negotiations from a position of some strength.

With the added confidence provided by a pre-shipment inspection, the client ended up as a happy customer with a proven source and a good deal.

- Toolkit: AIC, media, litigation checks; site visit; local sources; pre-shipment inspection.
- Conclusions: Due diligence is about positive business intelligence as well as negative risk identification and mitigation.

Private equity preliminaries

An international private equity business that had already developed a long list of over 40 investment candidates after an industry-wide research programme wanted to qualify and filter the targets for a shortlist before making direct approaches. Preliminary due diligence and market research was conducted over 10 days, and across more than 10 provinces, to confirm a defined set of criteria associated with the companies' operations, finances and development plans.

- Toolkit: Desk research, AIC, legal and media checks; site visits; sourced interviews with management, employees and industry contacts.
- Conclusions: Commercial due diligence can be usefully deployed during the research phase to filter out weak candidates, and ensure that options are kept in reserve. By deploying a range of specialist local resources in different parts of China, a high volume of work can be completed in a short period of time, and over a wide area.

Ethically challenged compliance

Investigation of health, safety and environmental issues in a Chinese mining group was ordered to assess ethical compliance risk on behalf of a foreign institutional investor. A review of legal and media records identified a number of issues. Further open-source analysis of the company's actions following historic incidents pointed to a lack of post-event compliance and a history of misleading statements. Sourced enquiries also suggested that questionable practices may have been employed by the company, and that there were previously unidentified compliance risks.

- Toolkit: Desk research; AIC, media and legal checks; social media and industry networks; sourced interviews.

- Conclusions: Due to the sensitive nature of some businesses and sectors, not all activities are transparent or reported, and the full picture requires sourced feedback from industry contacts, as well as review of official records and public information. Sustainability, corporate social responsibility and environmental issues are no longer optional extras for business in China.

Good dragon or bad dragon?
Source: Image by the author. 798 Art District, Beijing, 2007; Dragons are seen as powerful and auspicious in Chinese mythology, but generally as evil in the West

The Bad

It is not a bad thing to find problems when looking for them, even if it can be frustrating for the proposed deal. The bad news, when heard early enough, serves to inform good decision-making, and can save a lot of time and money. These Bad examples highlight:

- The need to see the big picture and for cross-reference of information
- Procurement fraud impact where processes are lacking
- The need for a Plan B when Plan A falls apart
- When something seems too good to be true, it needs a closer look

The foreign "Chinese" company

One investigation found that the target person, the registered owner of a Chinese company, passed the reputation checks without problem. The Chinese company also passed the relevant checks. However it was noted that the target spent a lot of time overseas, and had strong family links to one European country. Further investigation (including reference to the register of company directors in Hong Kong) showed not only that the target was a director a Hong Kong company but was also listed as being a foreign national—meaning that the original Chinese nationality must have been given up.

As a result the "Chinese" company was actually a foreign-invested one, and was improperly registered. That could have been a big risk for the client—a major international business for whom legal compliance had driven the due diligence process.

- Toolkit: AIC and online checks; covert site visit; pretext calls; reputation checks with customers and stakeholders; review and cross-checking.
- Conclusion: Every box may be ticked on the back of a positive check, but in the context of due diligence two positives can sometimes make a negative. Big-picture review, and cross-checking of details are essential, especially where local and international compliance risks are a concern.

Premium procurement

A large foreign company, with significant investments in China, instigated an investigation into corrupt procurement practices around a multi-million dollar project following a whistleblower's accusation of wrong-doing. The investigation found that there had been a complete lack of control around the procurement process, which had been handled by one senior individual, and that there had been no competitive tendering.

Benchmarking of product and service costs against a sample of invoiced items indicated that an average premium of over 5 per cent had been paid—suggesting that, at best, a significant amount of money had been wasted and, at worst, that senior management had defrauded the company. The lawyers took it on from there.

- Toolkit: Analysis of the commercial process; desk research; source interviews with suppliers and technical specialists, including mystery shopping for price comparisons.
- Conclusions: Internal fraud, including kickbacks in procurement, is a common risk in China. Processes, as well as checks and balances, need to be put in place to help ensure compliance. Whistleblowers are increasingly common but may sound the alarm too late.

Domain of chaos

Pre-acquisition due diligence into an internet-based Chinese service company showed that the business lacked clear processes and financial controls (not to mention a whole year's bank statements), and could not provide detailed transaction or payroll records. It did not however seem to lack fake fapiaos or a desire to avoid payment of appropriate taxes. The key asset of the business, and the reason for it being targeted, was its domain name. However, checks found that the domain was not registered to the company but to the company's owner. Needless to say, the transaction did not progress. On the bright side, the due diligence had been conducted in parallel with an alternative target, which (while not perfect) was in considerably better shape!

- Toolkit: AIC, media and legal checks; site visit and management interviews; review of financial and staff records; review of third-party information to confirm asset ownership.
- Conclusions: An online review of the business would suggest a reality quite different from the one experienced on the ground. Governance and compliance failures came to light based on site visits, staff interviews, and a lack of appropriate records. The founder's personal ownership of the main asset was a clear sign that he did not see the company as a separate legal entity but as a personal asset.

China buyer scam

Due diligence processes were used to uncover a "China buyer scam" (see the case study below), when a Chinese company approached a foreign supplier out of the blue and quickly made big "order"—but was considered more likely to be planning a fraud based on obtaining expenses and/or bribes to "facilitate" the conclusion of the non-existent deal.

- Toolkit: Commercial sense-check; AIC, media and legal checks; online searches for fraud references to the target.
- Conclusions: If a deal looks too good to be true (especially in a place as competitive as China) it probably is, and requires some due diligence. It may not be possible to prove bad intentions, but red warning flags should be taken seriously. A structured, research-based approach is needed in order to find qualified partners or customers. And if you get an email that looks like this one (which, by coincidence, just came in), simply move it to the scam spam folder:

"Dear Sir/Madam, We are interested in purchasing your products and we sincerely hope to establish a long-term business relation with your esteemed company. Please kindly send me your latest catalog. Also, inform me about the Minimum Order Quantity, Delivery time or FOB, and payment terms warranty. Your early reply is highly appreciated.

Thank You!
Best Regards,
Mrs Zhou [xxx], (Purchasing Manager), [xxxx] Co., Ltd."

CASE HISTORY: THE CHINA BUYER SCAM[1]

Sourcing from China comes with its own challenges, and a common one is "the China Buyer Scam." This is a scam which typically involves a newly set up Chinese company that contacts a foreign business with the bait of a large order. The Chinese company then requests the foreign party to visit and conclude the deal and/or tries to solicit additional payments for bribes or expenses. The unlucky (and overly trusting) foreign company gets very excited at the prospect of selling a big order to China, and is taken hook, line, and sinker. This scam reinforces the importance of due diligence for sellers as well as buyers. A simple and quick company analysis would help to see whether the company, and its import requirement, is genuine. It goes something like this:

1. International company (large or small) receives a big enquiry for their wonderful widgets. (Nice, but a bit strange these people appeared a bit randomly via the website, and that nobody has come across them before. Still, China is a new market, and things are all big and fast-moving...).

2. The enquiry rapidly turns into a firm order. (These guys seem really keen! It's also pretty impressive that they seem to have answers for all those boring technical questions. What's more, there was hardly any negotiation, which is great for the margin, but a bit of a surprise, as everyone says the Chinese are hard or price...)

3. The Chinese "buyer" invites the foreign firm to China to sign the contract on a tight schedule. (My, these guys are really moving fast. Better get the trip sorted out. But it would be good to know a bit more about them before I go...)

4. The unwary seller flies in to China—Yunnan, Guangdong, and Hainan are among the favourites—for the signing and a big dinner. (It is bloody cheeky that the buyer wants some cash for the event and/or a "commission"

payment to get the deal through in face of some internal politics—or whatever...)

5. The seller either then leaves in a strop, feeling it was a wasted trip or, worse, goes to the bank to get the money to ensure the deal goes through, and hands it over. (Where did everyone go?! Where is the money? What about the contract? Help!!)

Luckily many people listen to the inner voice that says "is this for real?" and, at around step 2 or 3, do some due diligence. Often the buyers do turn out to be from "real" (well, really registered) companies, but there are still red warning flags waving for those who care to look:

- Is the company just a few months old?
- Is it really ready to spend up to several million dollars?
- Has it got no verifiable trade references?
- Is it good on technical questions, but shaky on market knowledge?
- Is it based at an odd location for the industry or business type?
- Does the registered business scope match the current deal?
- Why is there no website (or a suspicious one)?
- Why don't they have any online listings to promote sales?
- Do questions from other potential suppliers appear in online business forums?
- And so on...

Still, when head office is suddenly keen to break into the China market (where have they been looking until now?), it is easy to overlook these things. And maybe the deal IS real! What then!?

In one case, a client's manager was scheduled to leave for China in a few days. He commissioned quick-fire due diligence report (there is never much time) on the buyer, and confirmed it was a real company. But the research also raised a number of the questions referred to above. It is difficult to give certain advice in an uncertain world (and stranger things have happened than an order arriving from a new Chinese company), but there were clearly risks (and in the worst-case scenario these could include personal security risks) and it was suggested the trip be reconsidered. Rather than just calling things off, a number of tactics were proposed—actions that might be usefully employed by anyone facing the dual pressures of temptation and trepidation in China:

- Delay the trip on a suitable pretext—The Chairman is making a sudden visit? In bed with avian flu? (Expect a request for commission payment).
- Invite the buyer to visit the overseas factory instead—and promise a good time. Of course, if they ask, the costs can be taken off the contract price as a sign of good faith. (No, sorry, the FD will not release any payment in advance.)
- Pass on a "request" from the overseas bank, which wants to speak with the buyer's bank on some boring procedural issues. (For some reason the Chinese bank will not respond.)

With a little poetic license, the client was prompted to propose that the official contract signing ceremony would be held at the British Embassy, with high-ranking officials in attendance. The response? The buyer emailed right back to say they had just signed the deal with another supplier. Given that the client was meant to be flying out the next day, for a deal worth in excess of US$10 million, it was clearly a scam. One that was thankfully avoided!

In another case, red flags were raised after visa invitation letters had been issued by a UK-based client to some prospective Chinese "buyers," but before the buyers had arrived in the country for negotiations. In that case it turned out the whole scam was just to get the visas. As is often repeated, it is a good idea to maintain healthy skepticism, treat China like other markets, ask questions and see if the answers make sense—and do some due diligence.

And, if everyone in the company is so excited about China all of a sudden—as a result of a random enquiry—take the opportunity to leverage that interest and do some structured market research. If there is a market opportunity it will be confirmed, and a sensible strategy can be agreed to take advantage of it. That route offers a much better chance of success (and employee-of-the-year awards) than jumping on a plane and parting company with a few thousand dollars.

The Ugly

Sometimes good times turn ugly, and damage-limitation is needed. In the best-case scenario losses can be recovered, or at least limited. But in many cases a lack of risk management means that nothing but a hard lesson can be taken away. Some of those Ugly lessons include:

- Risks that build over time, but which are not reviewed until too late
- Reliance on contacts (or contracts) is not enough
- A friendly face may hide an expensive foe
- Experience cannot always be effectively transplanted to China

Poisonous procurement

Procurement at a major foreign food company's China operations resulted in toxic ingredients entering the supply chain, and a significant financial loss together with damaging reputational impact. A lack of due diligence on key suppliers meant that the company was unaware of the level of subcontracting being used, who the subcontractors were, or what protections were in place. The investigation found that the supply chain had become extended over time and that, as profits dropped, shortcuts were taken and unsuitable additives brought in. As there was no regular due diligence or testing, the problem was not identified until it was too late.

- Toolkit: Site visit and management and staff interviews; procurement process analysis; AIC, legal and media checks on suppliers; interviews with industry sources and government officials.
- Conclusions: Due diligence is critical at the start of any important business relationship, but it must be updated on a regular basis to account for changing risks, for example as cost structures change. An upfront investment of a few thousand dollars can save millions in terms of recall costs and lost good will, and the whole-life cost of transactions (including the cost of potential liabilities) should be taken into account when considering the need for risk mitigation.

Contract recovery

In a long-running case involving an international trading company, a large Chinese company had failed to supply materials despite having received a multi-million dollar payment. The foreign company had previously relied on its solid relationship (the famed "guanxi" again) with the company's chairman but had been unaware he was being forced out. The new boss had no relationship and no inclination to deliver on the agreement. The case went to international arbitration outside China, and the foreign company won. However, when the award was presented for registration with the local Chinese court, it was rejected on a technicality. The Chinese rules, wary of local protectionism, require such rulings to be approved by the Supreme People's Count in Beijing, and the award was (finally) approved and passed back to the local court for enforcement. But by that time the Chinese business had been restructured and was left with no assets for recovery. Even some of the official records relating to land ownership had been "lost." Only with lobbying at local and central levels, and with the leverage gained from detailed investigations, was a compromise solution negotiated through the court, and some of the money recovered.

- Toolkit: AIC, media and legal and official documentation checks; company and transaction history analysis; cross-checking of shareholdings and executive roles; reputation checks; site visits; stakeholder and local source interviews and lobbying; specialist legal team.

- Conclusions: Connections can be as important as contracts, but neither offer full protection in cases of pre-payment. The legal system does not provide certainty, so risk management measures are needed in deal structuring. It is also important to maintain relationships on a regular basis and with a range of contacts.

The enemy inside

An overseas, family-owned business that was sourcing products from a number of suppliers in China suffered losses of millions of dollars due to their local representative in China taking kickbacks from suppliers over an extended period. An investigation found that the representative had also secretly established his own companies to supply the overseas company directly. The overseas owner had done no due diligence on the suppliers, so had no idea of their ownership until a whistleblower revealed the scheme. The company had to secretly diversify its supply chain before ridding itself of its long-time local representative (and his personal supply chain). They also hired a foreign lawyer to fix the problem, but having done no due diligence on him, soon found he was himself a fraudster, just out of jail!

- Toolkit: Desk and field investigations; AIC, media and legal reports; reputation checks; site visits, pretext calls and mystery shopping.
- Conclusions: Focusing too much trust on too few people is a big risk, especially where processes and due diligence are lacking. Losses to kickbacks and fraud may go unnoticed in a time of rapid growth, but the risk remains. As well as due diligence on direct suppliers, the whole supply chain needs regular, systematic review to ensure compliance and competitiveness.

fraud may go unnoticed in a time of rapid growth

Blind investment

A very wealthy and experienced foreign private equity investor put millions of dollars into an innovative service sector company in China, partly based on the impressive nature of the Hong Kong-based director, who claimed to be very successful and to have strong guanxi with the mayor of the city where the venture was based. As there were some concerns among the local investment team about the business and the Hong Kong director (whose public profile did not seem to match his personal claims), due diligence was recommended. However, the main investor vetoed it and pressed ahead with the deal. The questionable director then recommended and brought in a CEO to run the business, with no formal recruitment process or alternative candidates. Two years later red flags started to wave, and it turned out the director and CEO had been in collusion, and had been hiding the problems faced by the company. The company was eventually sold for a small fraction of the original investment.

- Toolkit: The toolkit in this case was not empty—all the necessary resources were available to the investor, but they remained unused.
- Conclusions: The experience and judgement that serve people well at home do not always travel well. Background and reputational due diligence could have highlighted shortcomings and identified conflicts of interest. A rich and powerful foreign investor may also not have the cultural sensitivity to see that a subordinate's polite suggestion that due diligence is needed may be a massive understatement of the risk.

Risky Business in Brief: The Good, The Bad and The Ugly

- *The due diligence toolkit is available; it just needs to be opened and used*
- *Proactive due diligence at the start of the process helps avoid or minimize risk*
- *Due diligence needs to be repeated on a regular basis, as risks change*
- *It can be valuable to bring in objective, independent risk analysis*
- *Risks don't just affect other people, so be prepared*

chapter 8

Conclusion: The New Reality

China is a market that few companies can choose to ignore. Its entrenched role as a manufacturing hub, combined with its emergence as a major consumer market makes it a prime target for businesses that are desperate for growth in a slowing global economy. It is no longer the case that China needs foreign capital, knowhow, and technology to accelerate its industrial development, and China no longer needs to offer tax breaks and other incentives to lure foreign firms in. It wants to develop and strengthen its domestic industries, develop national champions to serve its home market, and retain more of the value produced by its often low-paid workers, so that they can live Xi Jinping's "Chinese Dream."[1]

Below the surface, and some way from living the dream, China still suffers from huge inequality. Richard Brubaker of Collective Responsibility sees the increasingly risky wealth gap as a mega trend that businesses in China need to reflect on when considering the structural risks of the market. In the hospital sector, the scene of GSK's bribery and corruption scandal, low-paid doctors handling large budgets, and dealing with life-and-death situations are an obvious red flag. Factor in that patients feel so much frustration—even leading to serious violence against doctors[2]—and there is real moral hazard that goes well beyond regulatory compliance. Brubaker notes that Chinese citizens will continue to demand and drive change because of their individual aspirations, and as there is no general sense of acceptance when bad things happen—no belief in the socialist system that something terrible can be explained because "god willed it" as is the case in some parts of the world. This is partly the reason for the stunning change that has already been seen. The question is whether the change, ground-up and top-down, will continue at a fast enough pace.

A very focused Chinese government, with firm, long-term social and economic goals, and an increasingly assertive international voice, is feeling more pressure from the Chinese dreamers, and is putting more pressure on foreign business interests. The foreign multinationals have their purposes but also feed resentment that so much of China's hard work results in easy profits for foreign brands and foreign shareholders. This new reality requires foreign firms to pay much more attention to the social context, and to ensure that they can manage the increased political and regulatory risk. Sydney University's Kerry Brown describes today's foreign firms in China as being "supplicants who should indigenise and localise to create a Chinese strategy and identity." They should focus on what they contribute in terms of employment, technology and values, and avoid being perceived as mere profit extractors.

The slower the economic growth in China, the more foreign firms will be squeezed, and the more they will need to demonstrate their value as taxpayers and corporate citizens—or consider a tactical retreat. In explaining the pain felt by some foreign companies in China, Jeffrey Immelt, the CEO of General Electric, said in 2010[3]:

> It's getting harder for foreign companies to do business there … I really worry about China … I am not sure that in the end they want any of us to win, or any of us to be successful.

Many have reflected on those words, and many have tried to adapt. A few however feel that the rewards fail to balance the risks. Actavis, a major pharmaceutical company, announced its decision to pull out of the post-GSK China in early 2014.[4]

> Actavis made clear it views the risks in China as well beyond the potential benefits … Actavis' CEO Paul Bisaro stated "If we're

going to allocate capital, we're going to do so where we can get the most amount of return for the least amount of risk. And China is just too risky."

New structures and business models also need to be considered for the vast majority that remain for the long term. Some notable corporate moves have included minority, (previously avoided) joint-venture investments to leverage the power of local partners, strategic localization of operations to enhance operations and positioning, and outright sale to investors who can bring foreign brands to the market under Chinese ownership:

- Tesco has moved away from developing its own business in China, and opted for a minority, 20 per cent stake in a joint venture with state-owned China Resources Enterprises.[5]
- 3M has localized its business units, management and products, to be in China for China, and to "play as a local."[6]
- Weetabix avoided the challenge of foreign market entry when it was sold to a Chinese buyer, Bright Foods, which is hoping to leverage its domestic position to bring the brand direct to Chinese consumers.[7]

These companies are not alone in addressing change. As the political, legal and economic environment changes, "businesses are having to adapt their business models," according to McKinsey's David Cogman, and "inbound CEOs are having to catch up and clean up" as the outgoing ones end their typical three- or four-year China terms. These fresh CEOs mostly don't have tactical retreat as an option, and for some, wholesale restructuring is needed. China is simply too important to get wrong. Cogman advises that they get help from a team that is both China-experienced and China-capable—and that they do not make the mistake of jumping at the first offer of help, or relying on the "well-connected" person that is introduced as a fixer. And for those who sit back home in the boardroom "they need to get management teams on the ground to see things for themselves," and take a realistic view of what can and cannot be done and enforced within Chinese contract law. W. John

Hoffmann of XRG agrees, and suggests that a "corporate A-team" from HQ needs to take responsibility for the China operations. Unfortunately, most multinational executives lack real exposure to the China market environment. Furthermore, the experience of many corporate "old China hands" quickly falls out of date. Even big companies with impressive track records in China often lack the human continuity with which to sustain it. And just because a company does not have an operation in China does not mean China will not impact the business. As Hoffmann puts it:

> If there are any CEOs out there who think that their companies do not have a China risk, they are drinking their own Kool Aid! Nobody can afford to be complacent ... I am struck again, and again, and again by how companies that are regarded as world-class, global leaders, are humbled by mistakes they make in China.

Increasingly CEOs do get it, and PwC's Suwei Jiang points to the example of a large UK client with a mix of wholly owned and joint-venture investments in China. Despite not being a China specialist (or Chinese speaker), the company's CEO is in China every other month—realizing that such an important market cannot be run by corporate remote control.

Foreign companies operating in China have to adapt to the changing economic and political reality, and in particular to the risks arising from the crackdown on corruption. Hoffmann suggests that some foreign companies may need to either significantly restructure their operations, with a focus on both political and legal compliance, or else risk real trouble. Even those which restructure and root out corruption and regulatory problems may face serious difficulties. For those individuals and businesses which have come to depend on significant China-sourced cash-flow, a clean-up could promote a crisis for the network, for the people in the company, and ultimately for the company itself. "Foreign companies in China can be compliant with the law and still get screwed" if they fail to account for China's phenomenal dynamics and the impact of conditions outside the office walls," says Brubaker, who recommends that businesses need to move to global standards, consider divesting from China, or face a rising risk of failure. He cites the example of KFC, for which China has been a major profit source, where consumers demanded higher standards from a trusted brand (in a sector without much trust following milk powder and other scandals), and were unforgiving in the aftermath of the hormones-in-chicken scandal[8].

W. John Hoffmann, XRG[9]

In thinking about China, foreign companies need a holistic understanding of Chinese priorities, and to manage risk beyond the obvious borders of the deal or local business. Three kinds of (sometimes unexpected) risk need to be addressed when thinking about strategic risk management—pre- and post-impact:

- Icebergs: Visible risks that can be seen, in part. A common approach is to ask someone to map out the unseen bit below the surface with some due diligence. Impact can then be anticipated and hopefully, but not always, avoided.

- Black holes: Cataclysmic events (with potential for negative as well as positive impacts) that can change the world, and that cannot be dealt with by a linear risk analysis approach. A negative impact example is 9–11, while a positive one is the discovery of penicillin. Whatever the event, it will impact everyone.

- Flying garbage trucks: Inexplicable, blue-sky risks ... based on an actual event where a garbage truck landed on the roof of an apartment building in Hong Kong (think steep hills and winding roads). This sort of risk can be bad news, and it often gets worse. In the real-world case the crane that was sent to remove the garbage truck broke, and had itself to be rescued! It is impossible to foresee that sort of accident, but there needs to be a clear crisis plan to recover and/or to take advantage of the resulting opportunities. Unless somebody senior has responsibility for looking at both the likely positive and negative impact and implications of the unexpected event—right away—then nothing good is likely to come of it. It is only those companies who see and react to the positive opportunity of the unexpected who will be able to manage what comes next.

Risk management and due diligence in China need to be viewed in a holistic rather than a linear way, and it is not a simple question of process. There is no ten-point check list for this. But a system shock can create real opportunities for those that can recognize it and then react quickly.

Why do large companies make the same mistakes again and again? It is usually down to people, and lack of reflective learning from past transactions, because the knowledge is not absorbed into the organization. A Fortune 100 company may have three or four tough deals in China over a 20- to 30-year period, but the China deal expertise resides in the people who did the deals—who most likely have moved on—not in a static organization.

For CEOs who might want to do a quick, high-level check of their exposure to China, based on internal analysis, three questions may assist:

1. How big was revenue in China last year?
2. How big was revenue in the wider home market (such as NAFTA/EU) last year?
3. How many senior ("A-Team") managers are based in each geography?

Anecdotal results suggest that there is often an imbalance between the top people's location and the revenue source. Given the complexity of the China market, and its distance from corporate HQs, that should be a red flag for any board.

Just as high-level, political risks need to account for the per-sonalities at the top, so do the people employed on the ground need to be given serious consideration. Too many businesses delegate trust, and therefore China risk, to an individual, business partner, or local fixer. The delegation approach is simplistic, and does not allow business owners to take charge. Companies have to develop and deploy a corporate A-Team to get China right, and the CEO and board need to take own-ership—not just delegate responsibility, as the stakes are too high, and as China is different to everywhere else.

Human resources is a critical function in China risk man-agement, as people are key to compliance, and as their actions are driven by corporate targets as well as financial incentives. If the right balance of control and reward is not set up in the HR system, then it is unlikely that a balanced approach to risk will be taken by people when they hit the road in China. If the corporate system is predicated on revenue targets and closing deals, and does not recognize and reward the people who can say "no" to a deal, then it is fundamentally flawed. Unfortunately, most MNCs remain revenue and deal-driven.

Any risk review that does not account for how people are targeted and incentivized is missing a key part of the puzzle, as people are creative. If they are told to reach the a distant target, and that they will be well rewarded for doing so, they will find ways to get over the Chinese walls, corporate poli-cies, and any other barriers that are put in their way. They, like most companies, have their eye on the prize.

Firms struggle with intense competition in the supply chain, and the need to keep prices down in the marketplace. As a result they are often tempted to look past cut corners, and maintain the appearance of business as usual. Even after major recent bribery and corruption scandals, anecdotal reports suggest that behaviors are not changing on the ground. At a recent business event in China a foreign pharmaceutical executive was reported to have said that the best way to manage a whistleblower in China is to "send them abroad for an MBA." Given that the Chinese healthcare system faces such significant challenges, an army of ethically compromised MBAs is not likely to be the solution! In light of the huge financial, reputational, and consumer implications faced by companies who risk failing to meet the right standards in China, it is surprising that some big companies balk at the idea of spending a few thousand dollars and a bit of management time on developing impactful sustainability programs and matching corporate cultures. Brubaker suggests the risk of not investing, and of not moving "beyond compliance," could cost these companies billions of dollars in the future in terms of regulatory penalties, law suits, and lost sales. One problem he sees is that there is little vested interest in long-term business success or brand legacy. Too much short-termism means that there is little time for development of long-term thinking around sustainability, or development of governance or ethics. And for those that do try to move in that direction, the path is not an easy one.

Another reason to adapt is that high historic growth rates have slowed, and historic corporate results will be hard to sustain. Even past results probably do not reflect reality. Once the costs of regulatory fines, consumer recalls, and brand damage are factored in, the bank balance may be rapidly diminished. Brubaker calls for "the internalisation of externalities" such as regulation and supply chain risks. Instead of outsourcing costs (and associated risks), there will be increasing benefits from bringing them back in and controlling them, and for making business decisions based on the full cost (including future liabilities) rather than the more easily accountable invoice cost. If the business does not work in China on a full-cost basis, Brubaker recommends leaving now or changing the model. This is already happening to some extent, with the withdrawal of Actavis, and the move by some consumer companies to focus more on the value of service and experience than on simple product sales. Although many challenges remain, a more mature conversation is developing around the theme of sustainability in China. Rising costs, competition, environmental pressures, and regulation have resulted in thinner profits. A shallow talent pool means that companies increasingly have to offer an attractive working environment, not just good pay, to land the best people. More companies now see a real business case for sustainability and CSR programs, and the impact can be felt from hiring and corporate culture, to brand value and consumer engagement.

Fundamental political, economic, and social shifts have changed the nature of the opportunities and risks for foreign businesses in China. The country has emerged as the second largest economy in the world, and as an important driver of global growth with strategic political interests in the region and beyond. Domestically China is undergoing a significant reform program while managing a massive, urbanizing population that has social media as a tool with which to express increasingly vocal aspirations and frustrations. Entrenched local interests and state-owned enterprises are not the easiest targets for the Chinese government to deal with. But well-known foreign companies that are found, under scrutiny, to be flouting the law, abusing dominant market positions, or discriminating against Chinese consumers may be considered fair game. And the scrutiny is not only being applied within China. The reach of China's Anti-Monopoly Law review processes has extended to overseas M&A activity that could have an impact in the domestic market—just as the UK and the US authorities have sought to enforce foreign compliance rules on companies in China. China's dual position as a manufacturing base and a consumer market has made businesses increasingly reliant on it at both ends of the value chain. Costs have risen, helping turn workers into consumers but also putting dangerous pressure on supply chains, and on employees trying to achieve their challenging bonus targets—even if it might mean ignoring procedures and laws.

Foreign companies operating in China need to undergo a full review of risks in order to protect themselves from official scrutiny and the higher standards to which they are held. They also need to sustainably localize their business models in order to become part of the fabric of Chinese society, and valuable corporate citizens. Those that are new to China, or trading from abroad, including many smaller companies and those in emerging sectors, also need to put aside old assumptions about costs, and set up trusted (and verified) relationships that will help to deliver safe and secure products and services. Strategic leadership by CEOs, and deeper engagement by the boards of directors, can help to guide companies safely through the increasingly choppy waters. A focus is needed not only on the personalities driving change at the top of the Chinese government, and those implementing it at local levels—but also on the people employed by businesses, and the way in which they are hired, trained, targeted, evaluated, and rewarded.

Huge opportunities remain in China, but international businesses cannot afford to ignore the macro risks presented by changing regulatory and market forces. They should take long-term, protective measures that move beyond compliance processes and box-ticking due diligence, to incorporate a balanced approach to practical, on-going risk management, and to sustainable values and business models.

The Chinese leadership has set its course and is unlikely to change direction, so the exposure to risky business in China will only increase for those that do not take steps to align with the new reality.

Risky Business in Brief: The New Reality

- *China's attitude to foreign investment and foreign firms has cooled*
- *Corporate reliance on China as both production base and market increases risk*
- *Many foreign firms in China need to localize and restructure—or retreat*
- *Businesses should align HR, culture, targets, and incentives*
- *Due diligence is a protection, but foreign firms need to move beyond compliance*

What lies beyond ?
Source: Image by the author, on the Great Wall, Beijing, 2007

Appendix: Resources and Reads

Resources

There are a wide range of China-related business associations, and associated networks, to be found in most of the major economies. The following selections are noted below for reference:

- American Chamber of Commerce: www.amchamchina.org
- American/US–China Business Council: www.uschina.org
- Australia Chamber of Commerce: www.austcham.org
- Belgian Chinese Chamber of Commerce: www.bcecc.be
- Benelux Chamber of Commerce: www.bencham.org
- Belgian-Chinese Economic & Commercial Council: www.bcecc.be
- Brazil China Chamber: www.camarabrasilchina.com.br
- British Chamber of Commerce in China: www.britishchamber.cn
- Britain/China-Britain Business Council: www.cbbc.org
- Britain/The 48 Group Club: http://the48groupclub.com
- Câmara de Comércio e Indústria Luso-Chinesa: www.ccil-c.com
- Canada China Business Council: www.ccbc.com
- Canada China Business Council: www.ccbc.com
- China Council of the Netherlands Council for Trade Promotion: www.handelsbevordering.nl
- Comité France-Chine: www.comitefrancechine.com
- Cyprus-China Business Association: www.ccci.org.cy
- Danish Chamber of Commerce: www.dccc.com.cn
- Danish-Chinese Business Forum: www.dcbf.dk
- Deutsch-Chinesische Wirtschaftsvereinigung: www.dcw-ev.de

- Dutch-Chinese Chamber of Commerce: www.dccchina.com
  EU Chamber of Commerce: www.euccc.com.cn
- EU China Business Association: www.eucba.org
- Euro Chinese Center for Research & Development: www.eurochina business.com
- Europe China Research and Advice Network ECRAN: www.euecran.eu
- Finland-China Trade Association: www.kauppayhdistys.fi
- Fondazione Italia Cina: www.italychina.org
- French Chamber of Commerce and Industry in China: www.ccifc.org
- German Centre for Industry & Trade: www.germancentre.org.cn
- German Chamber of Commerce in China: http://china.ahk.de
- Hong Kong Chamber of Commerce: www.hkcccgd.org
- Ireland China Business Association: www.irelandchina.org
- Italian Chamber of Commerce: www.cameraitacina.com
- Japanese Chamber of Commerce and Industry in China: www.cjcci.biz
- Korean Chamber of Commerce: www.kochamsh.com
- Latvia–China Business Council: www.latviachina.eu
- Lithuania–China Trade Association: www.lcta.lt
- Maltese Chinese Chamber of Commerce: http://www.eucba.org
- Singapore Chamber of Commerce and Industry: www.singcham.com.cn
- Spanish Chamber of Commerce: www.spanishchamber-ch.com
- Sweden–China Trade Council: www.sctc.se
- Swedish Chamber of Commerce in China: www.swedishchamber.com.cn
- Swiss–Chinese Chamber of Commerce: www.sccc.ch

Reads

There are plenty of books for those who wish to dig deeper into the historical context, practical issues, and personal experiences associated with doing business in China. A few favourites and reading list targets (starting with a recommended three*, one from each section) include:

Big picture:

- China into The Future, Hoffmann and Enright
- China Shakes the World, James Kynge*

- China's Growth: The Making of an Economic Superpower, Linda Yueh
- China's Urban Billion: The Story Behind the Biggest Migration in Human History, Tom Miller
- Chinese Whispers: Why Everything You've Heard About China Is Wrong, Ben Chu
- The China Dream, Joe Studwell
- The Coming Collapse of China, Gordon Chang
- The Party, Richard McGregor
- Tiger Head, Snake Tails: China Today, How It Got There and Why It Has to Change, Jonathan Fenby
- When a Billion People Jump, Jonathan Watts

Business:

- China CEO, Fernandez and Underwood
- China Uncovered, Jonathan Story
- Doing Business in China, Chris Torrens
- Due Diligence in China: Beyond the Checklists, Kwek Ping Yong
- Guanxi for the Busy American; The Fragile Bridge, Andrew Hupert
- Managing the Dragon, Jack Perkowsky
- One Billion Customers, James McGregor
- Poorly Made in China, Paul Midler
- The 1 Hour China Book, Jeffrey Towson, Jonathan Woetzel*
- The End of Cheap China, Shaun Rein

Other:

- Adrift in China, Simon Myers
- Beijing Jeep, James Mann
- China Cuckoo: How I lost a fortune and found a life in China, Mark Kitto
- China Inside Out: 10 Irreversible Trends Reshaping China and its Relationship with the World, Bill Dodson
- Factory Girls, Leslie T. Chang
- Junkyard Planet: Travels in the Billion-Dollar Trash Trade, Adam Minter
- Mr. China, Tim Clissold*
- River Town, Peter Hessler

- Struggling Giant, Kerry Brown
- The China Price, Alexandra Harney

Online

- Company Data:
    - Hong Kong Integrated Companies Registry Information System (ICRIS): www.icris.cr.gov.hk/csci
    - State Administration of Industry and Commerce (SAIC): www.saic.gov.cn
- Courts and Credit
    - People's Bank of China's (PBOC) Credit Reference Centre: www.pbccrc.org.cn
    - Supreme People's Court's database of debtors: http://shixin.court.gov.cn
    - Supreme People's Court's court records: www.court.gov.cn/zgcpwsw
- Intellectual Property
    - China Trademark Office (CTMO): ctmo.gov.cn
    - State Administration of Industry & Commerce (SAIC): www.sbcx.saic.gov.cn
    - State Intellectual Property Office (SIPO): www.english.sipo.gov.cn
- Due Diligence Reports
    - Best Practices for Managing Compliance in China, US-China Business Council, October, 2013: http://www.uschina.org/sites/default/files/USCBC%20Compliance%20Report%202013.pdf
    - Due diligence for joint ventures, mergers and acquisitions in China, EU SME Centre: http://www.eusmecentre.org.cn/content/due-diligence-joint-ventures-mergers-and-acquisitions-china
    - Knowing your partners in China, EU SME Centre: http://www.eusmecentre.org.cn/content/knowing-your-partners-china
    - The China Business and Social Sustainability Check, Human Rights and Business Department of the Danish Institute For Human Rights: http://www.humanrightsbusiness.org/files/Publications/the_china_business_and_social_sustainability_check_dihr_uk_july_2009.pdf

Those that have an appetite for smaller bites of up-to-date news and views on China risk and due diligence issues can join the Risky Business in China LinkedIn Group (http://linkd.in/1fNWpNC) and follow @RiskyBizChina on Twitter. For social media and other links just scan the QR code below:

Notes

Introduction

1. Wikipedia, Foreign Exchange Certificates: http://en.wikipedia.org/wiki/ History_of_Chinese_currency#Foreign_Exchange_Certificates

1:   Opportunity and Risk

1. Tim Clissold, 2004 (Constable & Robinson)
2. Wikipedia: http://en.wikipedia.org/wiki/List_of_corporate_collapses_ and_scandals
3. Doing Business, China, 2014; IFC/World Bank: http://www.doingbusiness. org/data/exploreeconomies/china
4. Transparency International, Corruption Perceptions Index 2013: http:// cpi.transparency.org/cpi2013/results
5. Doing Business, China, 2014; IFC/World Bank: http://www.doingbusiness. org/data/exploreeconomies/china
6. 2014 Index of Economic Freedom, Country Rankings; http://www.heritage. org/index/ranking
7. Coface, 27 March, 2014, online Country Risk Assessment: http://www.coface. com/cofaweb/comparer/697-883-750-266. Note: Coface uses "a seven-level ranking. In ascending order of risk, these are: A1, A2, A3, A4, B, C and D".
8. Trust Barometer, 2014, Edelman; Slide 17: http://www.edelman.com/ insights/intellectual-property/2014-edelman-trust-barometer/trust-around-the-world
9. 2014 Index of Economic Freedom, Country Rankings: http://www.heritage. org/index/ranking

10. http://www.alixpartners.com/en/LinkClick.aspx?fileticket=oPZMj48fw9M%3d&tabid=635
11. Transparency International, Corruption Perceptions Index 2013: http://cpi.transparency.org/cpi2013/results
12. Trust Barometer, 2014, Edelman; Slide 17: http://www.edelman.com/insights/intellectual-property/2014-edelman-trust-barometer/trust-around-the-world

2:   How Risky Is Business in China?

1. US China Business Council: China Business Environment. Top Ten Business Concerns Identified by Companies (2013). https://www.uschina.org/reports/china-business-environment-october-8-2013
2. American Chamber of Commerce in China, China Business Climate Survey, 2013. Page 5 & 6, (top business risks & business challenges) http://web.resource.amchamchina.org/cmsfile/2013/03/29/0640e5a7e0c8f86ff4a380150357bbef.pdf
3. EU Chamber of Commerce in China, Business Confidence Survey, 2013. Business Challenges, page 12, figure 10 (top ranked business challenges) http://www.euccc.com.cn/en/publications-position-paper
4. EU Chamber of Commerce in China, Business Confidence Survey, 2013, page 4 http://www.euccc.com.cn/en/publications-position-paper
5. *China Daily*, February 17, 2014, Top 10 white-collar crimes of 2013: http://www.chinadaily.com.cn/business/2014-02/17/content_17287131.htm?utm_source=twitterfeed&utm_medium=twitter
6. *Caixin*, 18 February, 2014, Ending the Nightmare of Private Sector 'Crime': http://english.caixin.com/2014-02-18/100640208.html
7. Kroll, 2013/14 Global Fraud Report, China: http://fraud.kroll.com/interactive-map
8. Ernst & Young, 12th-Global-Fraud-Survey, page 14: http://www.ey.com/Publication/vwLUAssets/Global-Fraud-Survey-a-place-for-integrity-12th-Global-Fraud-Survey/$FILE/EY-12th-GLOBAL-FRAUD-SURVEY.pdf
9. In an interview with the author. China Accounting Blog: http://www.chinaaccountingblog.com
10. In an interview with the author; EU SME Centre: http://www.eusmecentre.org.cn. The Centre has written two due diligence reports, "Due diligence for joint ventures, mergers and acquisitions in China," and

"Knowing your partners in China." Registered users can download them via these links:http://www.eusmecentre.org.cn/content/due-diligence-joint-ventures-mergers-and-acquisitions-china; http://www.eusmecentre.org.cn/content/knowing-your-partners-china

11. In an interview with the author; EU SME Centre: http://www.eusmecentre.org.cn

12. In an interview with the author; Control Risks: http://www.control risks.com

13. Control Risks, Corruption/fraud and labour issues rank as top 5 business challenges in China: Annual survey, 3 April 2013: http://www.controlrisks.com/Media/ControlRisksDocuments/Corruption-and-labour-issues-top5-business-challenges-in-China.pdf

14. Xinhuanet, 1 March, 2014, China becomes world's largest goods trader: WTO: http://news.xinhuanet.com/english/china/2014-03/01/c_133152607.htm

15. Business Insider, 3 November 2011: http://www.businessinsider.com/exposure-to-china-integration-risk-2011-11

16. China Cuckoo: How I lost a fortune and found a life in China, Mark Kitto, Make-Do Publishing, page 96.

17. In an interview with the author; Cross Pacific Partner: www.crosspacific partner.com

18. In an interview with the author; Guanxi for the Busy American, Andrew Hupert (2012)

19. Coface, February 2014, Reality Check: Corporate Payment Trend And Sectorial Risk In China, page 5: http://www.coface.com/News-Publications/Publications/Reality-Check-Corporate-Payment-Trend-and-Sectorial-Risk-in-China

20. Adapted from: China: New Values in A Changing Society, Guy Olivier Faure, China Europe International Business School, Academia Sinica Europæa, Shanghai, Sorbonne, Paris V: http://www.ceibs.edu/ase/Documents/EuroChinaForum/faure.htm

21. Fang, 1999: 150

22. News of the Communist Party of China, 29 March, 2013, Communist Party of China in Brief: http://english.cpc.people.com.cn/206972/206981/8188392.html

23. *New York Times*, 26 June 2007, Murdoch's Dealings in China: It's Business, and It's Personal: http://www.nytimes.com/2007/06/26/world/asia/26murdoch.html?pagewanted=all&_r=0

24. *New York Times*, 11 April 2013, China's Former Rail Minister Is Charged With Corruption: http://www.nytimes.com/2013/04/11/world/asia/

liu-zhijun-former-chinese-rail-minister-charged-with-corruption. html?_r=0

25. Chinese Embassy, 5 November, 2006: China maps out informatization development strategy: http://www.china-embassy.org/eng/gyzg/t251756.htm

26. In an interview with the author

27. WSJ ChinaRealTime, February 12, 2014: Economists React: Is China's Export Boom Real?: http://blogs.wsj.com/chinarealtime/2014/02/12/ economists-react-is-chinas-export-boom-real/?mod=WSJBlog&utm_ content=buffer72c5d&utm_medium=social&utm_source=twitter. com&utm_campaign=buffer

28. Image by the author, Kunming, 2013

29. Beijing Jeep (p. 25), Jim Mann, 1989 (Simon and Schuster)

30. Strong Chinese white spirit

31. The Fragile Bridge: Conflict Management in Chinese Business, Andrew Hupert

32. Image by the author, "One World One Dream," The Great Wall, Beijing, 2007

33. Adapted from King & Wood's China Bulletin, Minimizing the Risks that Legal Representatives Face, January 2012: http://www.kingandwood. com/Bulletin/ChinaBulletinContent.aspx?id=7387ade2-757b-4552-b128-a6ad900230db

34. New York Times, 28 October 1998, Foreign Banks Move to Reassess Exposure: GITIC Bond Default Shakes China Creditors: http://www. nytimes.com/1998/10/28/business/worldbusiness/28iht-gitic.t_3.html

35. Wall Street Journal, 10 February 2014: Perils Mount As Debt Costs Swell in China: http://online.wsj.com/news/articles/SB100014240527023045588 04579374721862102300?mg=reno64-wsj&url=http%3A%2F%2Fonline.wsj. com%2Farticle%2FSB10001424052702304558804579374721862102300. html

36. Reuters, 13 February 2014: China trust sector reports slower growth; default risks in focus http://www.reuters.com/article/2014/02/13/ china-trusts-idUSL3N0LI2HX20140213

37. Reuters, 12 February 2014: China shadow-bank product defaults as coal company can't repay http://www.reuters.com/article/2014/02/12/ china-trust-default-idUSL3N0LH1L320140212

38. Quartz, 7 March 2014, China just had its first ever corporate bond default—and that's a good thing: http://qz.com/185297/china-just-had-its-first-ever-corporate-bond-default-and-thats-a-good-thing/

39. ChinaNews.com, 13 February 2014 (in Chinese): http://www.chinanews. com/gn/2014/02-13/5830511.shtml

40. In an interview with the author; Forensic Risk Alliance: http://www.forensicrisk.com

41. International Business Times, 29 July 2011, Yahoo got short end of stick in Alibaba deal: http://www.ibtimes.com/yahoo-got-short-end-stick-alibaba-deal-473388

42. Bloomberg, 15 December 2013: http://www.bloomberg.com/news/2013-12-15/baidu-forced-to-add-warnings-as-regulators-focus-on-china-stocks.html

43. Adapted from China Accounting Blog, FU shows VIE risk, 12 December 2013: http://www.chinaaccountingblog.com/weblog/fu-shows-vie-risk.html

44. Reuters, January 23, 2014, Special Report: How Caterpillar got bulldozed in China: http://www.reuters.com/article/2014/01/23/us-caterpillar-china-special-report-idUSBREA0M03720140123

45. McKinsey Quarterly, July, 2013: Due diligence in China: Art, science, and self-defense http://www.mckinsey.com/insights/corporate_finance/due_diligence_in_china_art_science_and_self-defense

46. China Stock Fraud, 16 November 2013, China Stock Fraud – Unknown Transactions!!: http://www.chinastockfraud.blogspot.ca/2013/11/china-stock-fraud.html

47. China Accounting Blog, 16 February 2014, List of Frauds: http://www.chinaaccountingblog.com/weblog/list-of-chinese-frauds.html

48. Reuters, June 6, 2011, Analysis: Muddy Waters is 5-for-5 on China short calls: http://www.reuters.com/article/2011/06/06/businesspro-us-china-stocks-muddywaters-idUSTRE7556D020110606

49. Financial Times, 17 December 2013: GSK China probe flags up wider concerns: http://www.ft.com/cms/s/0/ba26aa2c-6648-11e3-aa10-00144feabdc0.html#axzz2qaV7qC1v

50. Reuters, 19 July 2013, How GlaxoSmithKline missed red flags in China: http://www.reuters.com/article/2013/07/19/us-gsk-china-redflags-idUSBRE96I0L420130719

51. Reuters, 19 July 2013, How GlaxoSmithKline missed red flags in China: http://mobile.reuters.com/article/idUSBRE96I0L420130719?feedType=RSS&irpc=932

52. Financial Times, 24 July 2013, Bribery built into the fabric of Chinese healthcare system: http://www.ft.com/cms/s/0/9b8979e2-f45f-11e2-a62e-00144feabdc0.html?siteedition=uk#axzz2twk9cR7J

53. China Daily, 10 July 2007, Former SFDA chief executed for corruption: http://www.chinadaily.com.cn/china/2007-07/10/content_5424937.htm

54. New York Times, 30 March 2013, China Sentences Rio Tinto Employees in Bribe Case: http://www.nytimes.com/2010/03/30/business/global/30riotinto.html?pagewanted=all&_r=0

55. The Atlantic, 23 October 2013, China's Chilling Crackdown on Due Diligence Companies: http://www.theatlantic.com/china/archive/2013/10/chinas-chilling-crackdown-on-due-diligence-companies/280787

56. August 29, 2013, Peter Humphrey case shows effects of China's tightened privacy laws: http://www.ft.com/cms/s/0/ea96e13e-105a-11e3-99e0-00144feabdc0.html#axzz2sNAdqZEU

57. Wall Street Journal, 9 January 2013, Dun & Bradstreet Fined, Four Sentenced in China: http://online.wsj.com/news/articles/SB10001424127887323482504578230781008932240

58. The Compliance Blog, 5 November 2013, An Incriminating Board Decision of D&B in Violation of Chinese Privacy Law: http://www.complianceblog.net/Arc-v.Asp?ID=952

59. Bloomberg, 8 June 2012, China Limits Access to Company Filings After Short Selling Bids: http://www.bloomberg.com/news/2012-06-08/china-limits-access-to-company-filings-after-short-selling-bids.html

60. The Fraud Examiner, May 2013, How Fraud Investigation Just Got Harder in China: http://www.acfe.com/fraud-examiner.aspx?id=4294978054

61. South China Morning Post, 19 December 2012, CCTV report says KFC chickens are being fattened with illegal drugs: http://www.scmp.com/news/china/article/1107804/cctv-report-says-kfc-chickens-are-being-fattened-illegal-drugs

62. Wikipedia, 2008 Chinese Milk Scandal: http://en.wikipedia.org/wiki/2008_Chinese_milk_scandal

63. Danwei, 17 March 2005: Run Chicken Run http://www.danwei.org/newspapers/run_chicken_run.php

64. Reuters, 11 February 2014, Aston Martin recall highlights risk of China parts supply: http://www.reuters.com/article/2014/02/11/us-autos-aston-china-insight-idUSBREA1A0SD20140211

65. Wired, 2 December 2013, China's academic scandal: call toll-free hotlines to get your name published http://www.wired.co.uk/news/archive/2013-12/02/china-academic-scandal

66. New Scientist, 19 November 2012, Fraud fighter: 'Faked research is endemic in China' http://www.newscientist.com/article/mg21628910.300-fraud-fighter-faked-research-is-endemic-in-china.html#.UvKK1PmKUsA

67. China Daily, 10 April 2012, Nine stand trial for selling fake US degrees: http://usa.chinadaily.com.cn/china/2012-04/10/content_15008800.htm

68. Wall Street Journal, 18 July 2010, Chinese Debate Allegations of Fraudulent Credentials: http://online.wsj.com/news/articles/SB10001424052748703722804575369112701532990

69. CNN Money/Fortune, 2 December 2011, Controversy over ex-Google China chief: http://tech.fortune.cnn.com/2011/12/02/kai-fu-lee

70. BBC, 8 July 2001, Faking it as a foreign executive in China: http://www.bbc.co.uk/news/10462158

71. China Daily, 7 September 2010, Many airline pilots have fake credentials: http://www.chinadaily.com.cn/china/2010-09/07/content_11265252.htm

72. Xinhuanet, 2 July 2012, Apple pays 60 mln dollars for iPad trademark in China: http://news.xinhuanet.com/english/china/2012-07/02/c_131689488.htm

73. China Hearsay, 2 July 2012, Apple, Proview Settle on 60 Million for iPad Trademark http://www.chinahearsay.com/apple-proview-settle-on-60-million-for-ipad-trademark

74. China Law Blog, 14 July 2007, China Trademarks—Do You Feel Lucky? Do You? http://www.chinalawblog.com/2007/07/china_trademarks_do_you_feel_l.html

75. Financial Times, 8 August, 2013, China resources arm faces theft accusations: http://www.ft.com/cms/s/0/4e144596-fdbc-11e2-a5b1-00144feabdc0.html#axzz2vv46WPr0

76. The Economist, 19 April 2007, Wahaha-haha!: http://www.economist.com/node/9040416

77. Amazon, Beijing Jeep: http://www.amazon.co.uk/Beijing-Jeep-Study-Western-Business/dp/081333327X

3: Due Diligence in China

1. Quotations Book, Bruce Lee on Change: http://quotationsbook.com/quote/5744

2. Severe Acute Respiratory Syndrome (SARS), Wikipedia: http://en.wikipedia.org/wiki/Severe_acute_respiratory_syndrome

3. Adapted from China Law Blog, 12 February 2007, Let Me Tell You About China Due Diligence: http://www.chinalawblog.com/2007/02/let_me_tell_you_about_china_du.html

4. ©iStock.com, georgeclerk

5. New York Times, 30 March 2010, China Sentences Rio Tinto Employees in Bribe Case: http://www.nytimes.com/2010/03/30/business/global/30riotinto.html?pagewanted=all

6. China Law & Practice, March 2008: Investigative Due Diligence and M&A in China: http://www.chinalawandpractice.com/Article/1886201/Channel/9939/Investigative-Due-Diligence-and-M-A-in-China.html

7. In an interview with the author; www.McKinsey.com

8. In an interview with the author. Rupert Utley is a China-focused financial investigator.

9. Beijing Steele Business Investigation Center: www.china-investigation.com; Author of the (Chinese) book *Opportunities and Risks*

10. McKinsey China, 28 February, 2014, What we don't know about China: http://www.mckinseychina.com/what-dont-we-know-about-china

11. Eurasia Group, 6 January 2014, Eurasia Group Publishes Top Risks For 2014: http://eurasiagroup.net/media-center/view-press-release/Top+Risks+2014

12. China Daily, 25 November 2013 British PM to visit China in Dec: http://www.chinadaily.com.cn/world/2013cameronvisitcn/2013-11/25/content_17135498.htm

13. China Daily, 27 March 2014, China extends Airbus production venture, unblocks A330 deal: http://www.chinadaily.com.cn/business/2014-03/27/content_17382033.htm?utm_source=twitterfeed&utm_medium=twitter

14. China Daily, 27 March 2014, EU welcomes end of wine trade disputes with China: http://www.chinadaily.com.cn/food/2014-03/27/content_17383233.htm?utm_source=twitterfeed&utm_medium=twitter

15. APCO Worldwide: www.apcoworldwide.com

16. APCO Worldwide, 10 December 2010, China's 12th Five-Year Plan: http://apcoworldwide.com/content/PDFs/Chinas_12th_Five-Year_Plan.pdf

17. Brunswick, 13 November 2013, A Review of the Third Plenary Communiqué: http://www.brunswickgroup.com/media/229230/Brunswick-China-Analysis-CPC-Third-Plenary-Session-November-2013.pdf

18. Brunswick, 15th March 2014, A review of the Second Plenary Session of the 12th National People's Congress and the government's reform agenda: http://www.brunswickgroup.com/media/268332/Chinas-Annual-Political-Gathering-2014.pdf

19. 15 November 2015, Xi explains China's reform plan, Xinhuanet, http://news.xinhuanet.com/english/china/2013-11/15/c_132891949.htm

20. Exceptional Resources Group: http://www.xrg-china.com

21. CDN 5G2 – China 5th Generation Leaders: http://www.xrg-china.com/bro/XRG-CDN_5G2_Doc2-Overview.pdf

22. MOFCOM, 21 February 2012, Catalogue for the Guidance of Foreign Investment Industries (Amended in 2011): http://english.mofcom.gov.cn/article/policyrelease/aaa/201203/20120308027837.shtml

23. *China Daily*, 4 November 2004, Wal-Mart donate research center for Tsinghua: http://www.chinadaily.com.cn/english/doc/2004-11/04/content_388298.htm

24. *FinancialTimes*,8March2006,Chinaofficialwarnson'malicious'foreigntakeovers: http://www.ft.com/cms/s/0/ea14a16a-ae92-11da-b04a-0000779e2340.html#axzz2wJ8hKCe2

25. By the author, on China Business Blog, 15 March 2006, China, and the Story of the Malicious Foreign Takeovers: http://www.chinabusinessservices.com/china-and-the-story-of-the-malicious-foreign-takeovers

26. Freshfields, 16 August 2013, China's Anti-monopoly Law celebrates fifth anniversary: http://www.freshfields.com/en/knowledge/China%E2%80%99s_Anti-monopoly_Law_celebrates_fifth_anniversary/?LanguageId=2057

27. Lexology, 21 November 2008, China's MOFCOM imposes conditions on InBev's acquisition of Anheuser-Busch: http://www.lexology.com/library/detail.aspx?g=01db2126-5c27-4a6f-813e-a7406b6ff169

28. *Want China Times*: 3 March 2014, Beijing strengthens anti-trust enforcement: http://www.wantchinatimes.com/news-subclass-cnt.aspx?id=20140303000001&cid=1502&MainCatID=0

29. *Reuters*,19February2014,ChinaaccusesQualcommofovercharging,abusing dominance: http://www.reuters.com/article/2014/02/19/china-ndrc-idUSL3N0LO0MR20140219.

30. PwC China: Transfer Pricing in China: http://www.pwccn.com/home/eng/prctax_corp_transfer_pricing.html

31. Transfer Pricing Watch, 3 February 2014, Annual review: China and Hong Kong: http://www.transferpricingwatch.com/2263/annual-review-china-hong-kong

32. *Financial Times*, 3 May 2005, Fingers caught in the presses: http://www.ft.com/cms/s/1/680bffe6-bbf0-11d9-817e-00000e2511c8.html#axzz2utuKurTu

33. *Reuters*, 26 February 2014, Shanghai cracks down on booming taxi app market: http://www.reuters.com/article/2014/02/27/china-taxiapps-idUSL3N0LW0UR20140227

34. *Financial Times*, 26 March 2014, WTO orders China to dismantle 'rare earths' restrictions: http://www.ft.com/cms/s/0/962a0ba4-b4e6-11e3-9166-00144feabdc0.html?ftcamp=published_links%2Frss%2Fhome_us%2Ffeed%2F%2Fproduct&siteedition=uk#axzz2x5o9huOv

35. *Wall Street Journal*, 2 May 2012: What Bo Xilai's Downfall Means for You: http://online.wsj.com/news/articles/SB10001424052702304746604577379321481757202

36. In an interview with the author. PwC, www.pwc.co.uk
37. In an interview with the author; Fiducia Management Consultants: http://www.fiducia-china.com
38. China Solved, 16 October 2012, Negotiating to Win – The Curse of Strength: http://chinasolved.com/2012/10/negotiating-to-win-in-china-the-curse-of-strength
39. ©iStock.com, trait2lumiere
40. Shanghaivest: www.shanghaivest.com/en. Adapted from on an article "Are you sure you know enough about due diligence in China?" February 2014, also available at www.shanghaivest.com. Lui Kam has extensive experience of conducting due diligence and dealing with local accounting practices for international clients; Interviewed by the author.
41. Wikipedia: "Reports that say that something hasn't happened are always interesting to me, because as we know, there are known knowns; there are things we know that we know. There are known unknowns; that is to say, there are things that we now know we don't know. But there are also unknown unknowns – there are things we do not know we don't know". United States Secretary of Defense, Donald Rumsfeld; http://en.wikipedia.org/wiki/There_are_known_knowns
42. In an interview with the author; PTL Group: http://www.ptl-group.com
43. PTL Group, 24 April 2012, Operational Audit Lessons For Internal Control: http://www.ptl-group.com/blogs/en/operational-audit-lessons-for-internal-control
44. Warehouse Management Systems
45. Customer Relationship Management
46. In an interview with the author; Harris Moure: www.harrismoure.com
47. In an interview with the author; Mark Schaub is also author of "The Art of Law – Chronicling Deals, Disasters, Greed, Stupidity, and Occasional Success in the New China," 2007 (Kluwer Law International). Based on an interview with the author, February 2014.
48. King & Wood Mallesons: www.kwm.com
49. Adapted from: China Law Insight, 26 May 2010, Due Diligence Deal Killer or Deal Saver?:_http://www.chinalawinsight.com/2010/05/articles/corporate/foreign-investment/due-diligence-deal-killer-or-deal-saver
50. China Law Insight, 26 May 2010, Due Diligence Deal Killer or Deal Saver?:_Adapted from: http://www.chinalawinsight.com/2010/05/articles/corporate/foreign-investment/due-diligence-deal-killer-or-deal-saver

51. *Financial Times*, 5 June 2006, Big four firms plan boost to China staff: http://www.ft.com/cms/s/0/bdc9a522-f3ef-11da-9dab-0000779e2340.html#axzz2utuKurTu

52. Forensic Risk Alliance: www.forensicrisk.com

53. Reuters, 12 February 2014, China Units of Big-Four Firms Appeal Audit Ban: http://online.wsj.com/news/articles/SB10001424052702303704304579379410335942436?mg=reno64-wsj&url=http%3A%2F%2Fonline.wsj.com%2Farticle%2FSB10001424052702303704304579379410335942436.html

54. Independent Online, 18 March 2014, Alibaba loss shows Hong Kong needs change: http://www.iol.co.za/business/companies/alibaba-loss-shows-hong-kong-needs-change-1.1663162#.UyjGxfmKUsA

55. Growing Beyond: a place for integrity. Ernst & Young's 12th Global Fraud Survey, p. 23, China Adapted from: http://www.ey.com/GL/en/Services/Assurance/Fraud-Investigation---Dispute-Services/Global-Fraud-Survey---a-place-for-integrity---China

56. BBC, 14 February 2014, Avon may spend up to $132m to settle China bribery probe: http://www.bbc.co.uk/news/business-26184045

57. China Daily, 29 January 2013: Xi: Anti-graft drive will target both 'tigers and flies': http://www.cpcchina.org/special/cleanparty/2013-01/29/content_16184813.htm

58. US-China Business Council, October 2013, Best Practices for Managing Compliance in China: http://www.uschina.org/sites/default/files/USCBC%20Compliance%20Report%202013.pdf

59. Bloomberg, 8 December 2013, JPMorgan China Hiring Probe Spreads to Five More Banks, NYT Says: http://www.bloomberg.com/news/2013-12-08/jpmorgan-china-hiring-probe-spreads-to-five-more-banks-nyt-says.html

60. Global Association of Risk Professionals, 4 June 2013, The Risks of Doing Business in China: http://www.garp.org/risk-news-and-resources/2013/june/the-risks-of-doing-business-in-china.aspx

61. GreenbergTraurig: www.gtlaw.com

62. China Law & Practice, January/February, 2014, How to do FCPA due diligence on third party intermediaries: http://www.chinalawandpractice.com/Article/3297995/How-to-do-FCPA-due-diligence-on-third-party-intermediaries.html?LS=EMS970084

63. Ministry of Environmental Protection, The People's Republic of China: http://english.mep.gov.cn

64. Xinhuanet, 11 March 2008, China upgrades environmental administration to ministry: http://news.xinhuanet.com/english/2008-03/11/content_7766369.htm

65. ERM, 1 June 2010, China's History of Environmental Protection: http://www.erm.com/en/Analysis-and-Insight/ERM-Publications/Publications-Archive-2009---2010/Chinas-History-of-Environmental-Protection

66. Xinhuanet, 8 March 2013, China tackles environment issues through legislation: http://news.xinhuanet.com/english/china/2013-03/08/c_132218957.htm

67. Shanghaiist, 4 February 2014, Chinese government blows minds by releasing real-time factory pollution data: http://shanghaiist.com/2014/02/04/chinese_government_goes_real-time_o.php

68. In an interview with the author; Collective Responsibility: www.collective responsibility.org

69. China-Europe International Business School: http://www.ceibs.edu

70. In an interview with the author; ERM: www.erm.com

71. China Dialogue, China's Green Revolution, Energy, Environment and the 12th Five-Year Plan, Page 13: https://www.chinadialogue.net/UserFiles/File/PDF_ebook001.pdf

72. CleanBiz.Asia, 11 December, 2013: New regs make China impact assessments more transparent: http://www.cleanbiz.asia/news/new-regs-make-china-impact-assessments-more-transparent#.Uwx6t_mKUsB

73. NIMBY: "Not In My Back Yard"

74. The Guardian, 16 May 2013, Chinese protest at planned chemical plant over pollution fears: http://www.theguardian.com/world/2013/may/16/china-protest-chemical-plant-kunming-px

75. SynTao: www.syntao.com

76. China Labour Bulletin, 12 July 2013, Coal mine found to have concealed numerous deaths and accidents: http://www.clb.org.hk/en/content/coal-mine-found-have-concealed-numerous-deaths-and-accidents

77. China Labor Watch, 10 November 2010, COC: False Advertising of Disney: https://www.chinalaborwatch.org/pro/proshow-137.html

78. China Labor Watch, 15 October 2013, Mattel's Unceasing Abuse of Chinese Workers: An investigation of six Mattel supplier factories: https://www.chinalaborwatch.org/pro/proshow-183.html

79. China Labor Watch, 4 September 2012, An Investigation of Eight Samsung Factories in China: https://www.chinalaborwatch.org/pro/proshow-177.html

80. China Labour Watch: www.chinalaborwatch.org
81. China Real Time, 29 July 2013, Apple's Response to Latest Supplier Labor Abuse Allegations: http://blogs.wsj.com/chinarealtime/2013/07/29/apples-response-to-pegatron-worker-allegations
82. China Labor Watch, 27 July 2012, Beyond Foxconn: Deplorable Working Conditions Characterize Apple's Entire Supply Chain: https://www.chinalaborwatch.org/pro/proshow-176.html
83. China Labor Watch, 27 July 2012, Beyond Foxconn: Deplorable Working Conditions Characterize Apple's Entire Supply Chain (pp. 8–9): https://www.chinalaborwatch.org/pro/proshow-176.html
84. The Human Rights and Business Department of the Danish Institute for Human Rights, 2009, China Business and Social Sustainability Check: http://www.humanrightsbusiness.org/files/Publications/the_china_business_and_social_sustainability_check_dihr_uk_july_2009.pdf
85. McKinsey Quarterly, 2013, Number 3, China's Next Chapter, Page 138: https://s3-ap-northeast-1.amazonaws.com/mckinseychinavideos/PDF/mckinsey_quarterly_chinas_next_chapter.pdf
86. In an interview with the author
87. The Risk Advisory Group, 6 February 2013, Can You Do Effective Due Diligence in China?: http://news.riskadvisory.net/index.php/2013/02/due-diligence-in-china
88. In an interview with the author; Kelly Services: http://kellyservices.cn
89. In an interview with the author; Heidrick & Struggles: www.heidrick.com
90. Reuters, 25 February 2014, LinkedIn jumpstarts China expansion with Chinese language site: http://www.reuters.com/article/2014/02/25/us-linkedin-china-idUSBREA1O00620140225

4: Putting Due Diligence on the Map

1. Twitter, February 2014
2. Twitter.com, February 2014
3. China Business Blog and @ChinaBlogTweets are edited by the author
4. Wikipedia, Feng Shui: http://en.wikipedia.org/wiki/Feng_shui
5. Silk Road International Blog, 12 February 2013, Are You performing The Ferrari Test?: http://silkroadintl.net/blog/2013/02/12/are-you-performing-the-ferrari-test

5: Survival Toolkit

1. In an interview with the author; Sofeast: www.sofeast.com
2. Sofeast, 3 July 2012, What questions can you ask a Chinese factory during a visit?: Adapted from: http://www.qualityinspection.org/questions-chinese-factory/
3. Ministry of Commerce of the People's Republic of China, Contact Method of the Local Administration: http://english.mofcom.gov.cn/article/topic/chinainvest/localguide/200702/20070204378447.shtml#14
4. National Law Review, 19 February 2014, New People's Republic of China (PRC) Policies on Annual Inspection: http://www.natlawreview.com/article/new-people-s-republic-china-prc-policies-annual-inspection
5. China Law Blog, 19 November 2013: China Contracts: Is That A Real Seal/Chop?; 26 January 2014, China Contracts: Is That A Real Seal/Chop? Part II; Adapted from: http://www.chinalawblog.com/2013/11/china-contracts-is-that-a-real-sealchop.html & http://www.chinalawblog.com/2014/01/china-contracts-is-that-a-real-sealchop-part-ii.html
6. TechInAsia, 19 February 2013, A Shocking Expose of China's Black PR Industry Implicates Government Officials, is Quickly Deleted from the Web: http://www.techinasia.com/caixin-posts-shocking-expose-chinas-black-pr-industry-story-quickly-deleted-web
7. Xinhuanet, 27 November 2013: Chinese courts publish judgement documents online: http://news.xinhuanet.com/english/china/2013-11/27/c_132923578.htm
8. EU SME Centre, 12 September 2013, Knowing Your Partners in China: http://www.eusmecentre.org.cn/content/knowing-your-partners-china
9. Muddy Waters, 2 February 2011, The Six Rules of China Due Diligence: http://www.muddywatersresearch.com/2011/02/six-rules-china-due-diligence
10. China Law Blog, 8 February 2011, The Seven Rules of China Due Diligence, adapted from: http://www.chinalawblog.com/2011/02/the_seven_rules_of_china_due_diligence.html
11. King & Wood Mallesons, 26 May 2010, adapted from Due Diligence Deal Killer or Deal Saver? http://www.chinalawinsight.com/2010/05/articles/corporate/foreign-investment/due-diligence-deal-killer-or-deal-saver
12. Fiducia Management Consultants, Issue III 2013, The 7 Rules for a Successful Acquisition: http://www.fiducia-china.com/china-insights/china-focus/newsletter/2013/fiducia-china-focus-issue-3/-2013/the-7-rules-for-a-successful-acquisition

13. Human Rights and Business Department of the Danish Institute for Human Rights, The China Business and Social Sustainability Check, July 2009: http://www.humanrightsbusiness.org/files/Publications/the_china_business_and_social_sustainability_check_dihr_uk_july_2009.pdf

6:   Emergency Services

1. http://www.moj.gov.cn/index/content/2013-08/22/content_4787444.htm
2. China Law & Practice, November/December 2013, Freshfields and Fangda triumph at CLP awards: http://www.chinalawandpractice.com/Article/3255184/Search/Freshfields-and-Fangda-triumph-at-CLP-awards.html?Keywords=CLP+Awards+2013
3. *Financial Times*, 16 April 2013, Accounting: Stalking the Big Four: http://www.ft.com/cms/s/0/cd74664e-9797-11e2-97e0-00144feabdc0.html#axzz2sNAdqZEU
4. *China Daily*, 26 August 2013, Big Four accounting firms no longer biggest: http://www.chinadaily.com.cn/business/2013-08/26/content_16920845.htm
5. *China Daily*, 26 August 2013, Big Four accounting firms no longer biggest: http://www.chinadaily.com.cn/business/2013-08/26/content_16920845.htm
6. China Accounting News Weekly [No.194], 22–28 June 2013, The public announcement of 100 accounting firms in 2013: http://www.chinaac-counting.cn/news/2013/0628/91864.shtml
7. Accountancy Age, 8 July 2013, Top 35 Networks 2012: The Survey: http://www.accountancyage.com/aa/feature/2280076/top-35-networks-2012-the-survey

7:   The Good, the Bad, & the Ugly

1. Adapted from China Business Blog, How to Scupper a Scammer: Adapted from: http://www.chinabusinessservices.com/how-to-scupper-a-scammer

8: Conclusion: The New Reality

1. *China Daily*, 8 December 2013, Experts interpret the Chinese Dream: http://www.chinadaily.com.cn/china/2013-12/08/content_17159773.htm. "The Chinese Dream – put forth by Xi soon after he ascended to China's top leadership position in November 2012 – calls for realizing a moderately prosperous society, national rejuvenation and people's happiness."
2. BBC, 28 February 2014, China sees wave of violence against hospital staff: http://www.bbc.co.uk/news/world-asia-china-26364133
3. Wall Street Journal, China Real Time, July 2, 2010: http://blogs.wsj.com/chinarealtime/2010/07/02/immelt-on-china-they-wont-let-us-win
4. *Forbes*, 3 February 2014, Why Did One of The World's Largest Generic Drug Makers Exit China?: http://www.forbes.com/sites/benjaminshobert/2014/02/03/why-did-one-of-the-worlds-largest-generic-drug-makers-exit-china
5. The Guardian, 9 August 2013, Tesco set to withdraw brand from China in new joint venture: http://www.theguardian.com/business/2013/aug/09/tesco-withdraws-brand-china-joint-venture
6. CKGSB Knowledge, 13 February 2014, 3M Company: In China For China: http://knowledge.ckgsb.edu.cn/2014/02/13/china/3m-company-china-china
7. *The Guardian*, 3 May 2012, Bright Food is betting on the Chinese falling in love with Weetabix: http://www.theguardian.com/business/nils-pratley-on-finance/2012/may/03/bright-food-bet-chinese-weetabix
8. Market Watch, 5 February 2013, Yum Brands investors choke on China chicken crisis: http://blogs.marketwatch.com/thetell/2013/02/05/yum-brands-investors-choke-on-china-chicken-crisis
9. In an interview with the author; Exceptional Resources Group: http://www.xrg-china.com
10. Image by the author, on the Great Wall, Beijing, 2007

Index

Printed and bound by CPI Group (UK) Ltd, Croydon, CR0 4YY